JR-02

Discovering What Schools Really Teach

Designing Improved Coursework Indicators

Lorraine M. McDonnell, Leigh Burstein, Tor Ormseth, James M. Catterall, David Moody

June 1990

Prepared for the
Office of Educational Research
and Improvement,
U.S. Department of Education

PREFACE

This policy guide argues the case for improved indicators of student coursework, illustrates the kinds of information they convey, and assesses the feasibility of alternative data collection strategies for producing them. It is not a typical research report summarizing study findings in full detail, nor is it a handbook for technical experts charged with designing new indicators. Rather, the guide is addressed to members of the policy community who use the information generated by state data systems and who must decide on the value and feasibility of gathering additional data. A companion to this volume, *The Design of Improved Coursework Indicators: First Steps,* Center for Research on Evaluation, Standards, and Student Testing (CRESST), UCLA Graduate School of Education, explores the technical issues involved in designing coursework indicators and is primarily intended to be used by those who develop new measures and manage data collection, analysis, and reporting.

This policy guide was prepared as part of a project sponsored by CRESST and funded by the Office of Educational Research and Improvement (OERI), U.S. Department of Education.

SUMMARY

What is taught, who teaches, and how they teach lie at the heart of schooling. Yet the development of improved curriculum measures has lagged far behind that of school resource and student achievement measures. Current indicators are inadequate and will become even more so as curricular policy and practice evolve.

WHAT IS COURSEWORK?

Coursework is the most tangible feature of curriculum at the high school level. Although coursework does not encompass the full range of ideas, values, and knowledge that schools attempt to inculcate in students, it does capture essential elements of curriculum that can be measured in a systematic way. In its broadest form, coursework includes the courses that schools offer, patterns of coursetaking by different types of students, the content of those courses, coursework objectives, the instructional strategies used, and teachers' qualifications and experience.

This policy guide argues the case for improved indicators of student coursework, illustrates the information different types of measures convey, and outlines the key choices that need to be made about data collection strategies. The examples used in the text are drawn from the School Reform Assessment (SRA) project, a two-year exploratory study undertaken to design a variety of coursework indicators.

THE CASE FOR IMPROVED INDICATORS OF STUDENT COURSEWORK

The need for better coursework indicators can be argued on both educational research and policy grounds. Research on the relationship between student achievement and coursework has shown that data on student test scores are of little use unless information is also available on factors that influence the distribution of those scores and help shape changes in achievement, for example, the curricular opportunities afforded different types of students. But that information must consist of more than course offerings and enrollment statistics enumerated simply by course title. Many course titles convey no information about content or how that content is presented. Because the curriculum offered within most high schools is differentiated according to student ability levels, and curricula also vary significantly across schools, course titles tell very little about what the schools are teaching or how coursework is influencing student performance.

Over the past decade, elected officials, especially at the state level, have extended their traditional concern about how schools are governed and financed to include what the schools teach, who teaches it, and in some cases, how it is taught. Policymakers are now interested in learning about the content students are receiving, and many have expressed concern about the effects of recent coursework policies on low-achieving students and on the range of curricular offerings. Current data, based on simple enrollment counts, is inadequate to answer their questions. Indicator designers will increasingly have to take into account both the broader schooling context in which curriculum is delivered to students and the question of depth as well as breadth of coverage. Even states with well-developed indicator systems lack data beyond course enrollment statistics, and more sophisticated data are limited to national samples.

DESIGN STANDARDS FOR COURSEWORK INDICATORS

Indicators that validly measure which courses schools offer, the content included in those courses, the qualifications of the people teaching them, and the students enrolled in them must meet four technical criteria:

- They must be linked to a larger model of the schooling process.
- They must differentiate among tracks or levels of the curriculum.
- They must distinguish between the curriculum as it is intended by designers and policymakers and as it is actually implemented in schools and classrooms.
- They must measure, to the extent possible, the depth of the curriculum as well as its breadth.

Coursework indicators, however, must meet more than just technical standards. To be policy-relevant, they must also provide useful information for policy decisionmaking, and they must be feasible to collect and report.

SAMPLE COURSEWORK INDICATORS

Student coursework consists of four basic elements: content or topic coverage, instructional strategies, curricular objectives, and teacher qualifications. Valid coursework indicators can help gauge how schools perform on each of these dimensions.

Topic Coverage

Coursework patterns and trends can be identified by asking teachers to note how many class periods they devoted to a particular topic in a specific section and how they treated that topic. Topic coverage data can be used in a variety of ways. Reports of the average number of periods across classrooms and schools, for example, enable comparisons of the proportion of class time spent on formal institutions in U.S. government classes as opposed to the proportion spent on political dynamics and policy outputs. Or they can be used to examine how the relative emphasis accorded different topics compares with state curriculum frameworks and various professional standards, or how this emphasis has changed over time.

One measure of the quality of a high school curriculum is the amount of an academic subject's core content that is covered in a typical course and whether that proportion varies significantly across sections of the same course. Sophisticated indicators can be constructed from topic coverage data to show the proportionate coverage of core topics in different types of classes. For example, data from a small sample of schools in the SRA project showed that while students in a typical algebra I section had more exposure to a core set of algebra and enriched topics than their counterparts in either pre-algebra or general mathematics classes, content coverage varied enormously across sections of courses with the same title. Excluding extreme values, the proportion of topics covered ranged from 44 to 93 percent in algebra I sections; from 33 to 80 percent in pre-algebra; and from 0 to 67 percent in general mathematics sections. In other words, topic coverage data revealed that in this sample of schools, some algebra I students receive no more exposure to algebra content than students enrolled in general mathematics and pre-algebra classes.

Instructional Strategies

Information about the mode in which content is being delivered to students can be obtained by asking about the frequency with which teachers use different instructional strategies (e.g., lecturing to the class, having students work in small groups, assigning research papers, etc.). Information about instructional strategies can provide important insights into the curricula that different types of students are receiving. For example, while the teacher lectured almost every day in U.S. history and government classes of all ability levels in the indicator design sample, more than twice as many high- and average-ability classes than low-ability classes required student presentations at least monthly, and students in high-ability classes were three times as likely as those in low-ability classes to write research papers.

Curricular Objectives

The relative emphasis teachers place on different objectives (e.g., developing an attitude of inquiry vs. performing computations with speed and accuracy) is an indicator of their expectations for a particular course, and their choice of objectives is likely to influence how they configure topics and instructional activities within that course. Teachers' reported objectives can thus suggest the direction in which coursework and teaching in a particular subject area may be heading. And, like topic coverage and instructional activities, the relative emphasis accorded different objectives also helps in differentiating among course levels—e.g., an overwhelming majority of general mathematics teachers in the SRA sample reported a major emphasis on developing an awareness of the importance of mathematics in everyday life, while significantly more algebra I teachers listed cultivating a systematic approach to problem-solving as a major emphasis in their classes.

Teacher Qualifications

A final indicator of student coursework is the match between teachers' qualifications and their teaching assignments. States are increasingly collecting teacher assignment data that can be linked to a database on teacher certification status. However, certification status in some subjects may provide only a partial, or even a distorted, picture of teacher qualifications. For example, 83 percent of the 310 mathematics sections in the SRA sample were taught by teachers certified in mathematics, but only 58 percent were taught by teachers who had majored in mathematics or mathematics education. Years of teaching experience and the recency of professional development in relevant subject matter are two other measures of teacher qualifications.

DATA COLLECTION STRATEGIES FOR COURSEWORK INDICATORS

The tradeoff between ensuring high technical quality of indicators and minimizing cost and respondent burden becomes clearest when indicator system designers have to decide which data collection strategies to use. States and school districts that currently collect information on coursework typically use the least expensive and least burdensome option, that of recording school-level offerings and enrollment categorized by conventional course titles. However, as the technical limitations of these data grow more apparent and policymakers continue to demand better information, states will have to adopt data collection strategies that entail greater cost and respondent burden but produce more valid and useful information. Although in-depth methods such as classroom observations will never be feasible for collecting routine indicator data, teacher surveys, combined with periodic collection of more detailed data, may be a reasonable alternative.

In most subject areas, teacher surveys will require several years to design, and each will take from 30 minutes to 1 hour to fill out. However, the costs of initial design work can be reduced if states and school districts form consortia to share responsibility for development efforts. Teacher burden can be minimized by collecting coursework data only once every two or three years, by focusing on only several critical courses in each subject area, and by collecting data in cycles, for example, covering English and social studies in one cycle and mathematics and science in the next.

Ensuring the validity of the inferences drawn from indicator data requires that benchmark data be collected. These data are more difficult and costly to collect than routine indicator data, and they serve as standards or anchors against which the validity of the routine data can be judged. Benchmark data require deeper probes than are possible with survey data and, as such, do not need to be collected as often or on as large a sample as conventional indicator data.

Benchmark data can serve four purposes in a state indicator system:

- Benchmark data can inform the development and evaluation of new coursework measures because they represent the content and process of instruction much more closely than do more routine data (e.g., in-depth interviews with teachers or classroom observations vs. teacher surveys), and they are less subject to the extraneous influences that limit or compromise routine data.
- After an indicator system has been operating for some time, benchmark data can be used to assess the extent to which measures have been corrupted by social desirability or policy pressures (e.g., teachers reporting classroom behaviors consistent with reform policies, while their examinations do not reflect such behaviors).
- Benchmark data can provide a context for interpreting trends or unexpected changes in aggregate indicator data (e.g., through school-level case studies).
- Benchmark data can be used to complement and enhance indicator system data through studies that explore in depth areas of policy or practitioner concern that indicator data have signaled as problematic (e.g., curricular opportunities becoming more unequal in certain types of schools).

We recommend that states interview small samples of district- and school-level staff, code student transcripts, and review teachers' syllabi and course materials. We also recommend that states wishing to collect more extensive data on student coursework make significant and continuing investments in benchmark data. About one-quarter of a state's coursework indicator budget should be allocated to benchmark data collection.

AVOIDING PROBLEMS IN THE USE OF COURSEWORK INDICATORS

Those who commission and design new indicators can rarely control how they are used. Nevertheless, taking into account how similar measures have been used in the past and anticipating how new ones might be used could help to avoid problems. State officials should keep in mind, first, that as indicators gain significance in the policy world, they tend to provide less valid information about what is actually occurring in classrooms—that is, they are likely to become corrupted as measures. Second, indicators are powerful levers for changing classroom behavior, but the changes are often not what policymakers and indicator designers intended.

Such problems can be minimized if state officials are clear from the very beginning about the appropriate uses of coursework indicators. These indicators are best used to document trends, assess the performance of the overall educational system, identify and target policy solutions, and aid in local improvement efforts. If they are used to compare schools or to assess teacher performance, they will probably cease to provide valid information and may even distort instructional practices in ways that compromise student learning.

CONCLUSIONS

Improving the information base on which decisions are made about educational policy and practice is not easy. Designing valid and useful measures takes time; collecting the necessary data imposes financial and other costs; and using indicator data in a constructive way requires considerable thought and planning. While these represent formidable challenges in any type of indicator development, they are particularly demanding in the case of coursework indicators because of the need for validation and deeper probes in the form of benchmark data.

Despite these challenges, the price that states will pay for not collecting better coursework data may be unacceptably high. Strategies for attaining performance goals cannot be implemented, classroom learning opportunities cannot be equalized, and policy impacts cannot be effectively monitored if current information gaps persist. Indicator development will never have the visibility or political appeal of new policy initiatives aimed at improving schools. Nevertheless, data about what schools are teaching form the cornerstone of those initiatives, and the constituents of public schooling need valid information on coursework to continue the work of educational reform.

ACKNOWLEDGMENTS

At every stage of this project, we have benefited from the expert counsel of UCLA colleagues Eva Baker and Joan Herman and RAND colleague Daniel Koretz. Larry Gess of the Georgia State Department of Education and Carvin Brown of the University of Georgia graciously assisted us in identifying and gaining access to several Georgia high schools. Kathy Rosenblatt and Pat Damiano coded the student transcripts with care and accuracy, and Zhen Chen and Lin Li handled computer programming tasks for the study.

Reviews by Jeannie Oakes of UCLA, Pascal Forgione of the Connecticut State Department of Education, and Brian Stecher of RAND helped us sharpen our ideas and communicate them more clearly. Janet DeLand's skillful editing and Marilyn Gerbi's efforts in preparing the manuscript are much appreciated.

We are particularly grateful to the classroom teachers, principals, counselors, and students who allowed us to use their schools to pilot a data collection strategy for producing coursework indicators, and who helped us understand the complexity of measuring what schools really teach.

CONTENTS

FIGURES

TABLES

1. THE NEED FOR IMPROVED INDICATORS OF STUDENT COURSEWORK

While no single theme characterizes the education reforms of the past five years, two predominate. The first is an emphasis on curriculum: what students study; what skills, concepts, and knowledge are included in their course of study; and who teaches them. This emphasis resulted from growing concern that American students are not receiving as rigorous a curriculum as their counterparts in nations that compete economically with the United States, and from evidence that learning opportunities are unequal across different types of local districts, schools, and students. Policy actions addressing these concerns have included increased course requirements for high school graduation; state and local guidelines for core curricula; efforts to improve the quality of textbooks; and greater attention to the match between teacher qualifications and teaching assignments.

THE DEMAND FOR BETTER INFORMATION

The second theme is a demand for better information about the schooling process and its outcomes. This demand is premised on the belief that schools should be held accountable to the public and to their elected representatives and that sound information about educational conditions and performance is critical to improving the quality of schooling. Policies designed to meet this need have included the expansion of state testing programs; the upgrading of state indicator systems to encompass measures beyond student scores on standardized tests; and a variety of programs that reward, punish, or assist schools based on indicator data.

This policy guide joins the two themes by suggesting ways in which states might develop more valid and useful indicators of student coursework. At the high school level, coursework is the most tangible feature of curriculum, defined here as the complete array of learning opportunities provided to students throughout their years of schooling. Although the notion of coursework does not encompass the full range of ideas, values, and knowledge that schools attempt to inculcate in students, it does capture most of the essential elements of curriculum that can be measured in a systematic way. In its broadest form, coursework includes the courses that schools offer, patterns of coursetaking by different types of students, the content of those courses, coursework objectives, the instructional strategies used, and teachers' qualifications and experience.[1]

[1]This report focuses on high school curricula because the notion of coursework is well-defined at that level. Curricular content in elementary schools is not as clearly divided into separate courses, and instructional groupings operate at the level of the work group rather than the entire classroom; therefore, curriculum indicators need to be conceptualized and measured differently at that level. Section 6 discusses these distinctions and their implications for designing indicators of the curriculum presented to different types of elementary school students.

The strategies and recommendations discussed here are based on an exploratory project undertaken to develop reliable coursework indicators that are also:

- Sensitive to major policy changes,
- Relevant to policymakers' information needs, and
- Efficient to collect and report.

This guide does not outline step-by-step procedures for designing new indicators. Not only was our research too preliminary to produce a document of such certainty, but each state will have to tailor its indicators to its own policies, instructional practices, and information needs.

Although the design strategies we present are suggestive, we argue strongly that indicators of student coursework are needed and that current measures are inadequate and will become even more so as curricular policy and practice continue to evolve over the next decade. The remainder of this section presents a case for improved indicators of student coursework. Section 2 discusses the characteristics of valid and useful coursework indicators. Section 3 briefly summarizes the research project on which this guide is based. Section 4 presents sample coursework indicators and illustrates the kinds of information they can provide. Section 5 assesses different strategies for collecting data on student coursework. Finally, Section 6 outlines steps that states can take to develop improved coursework indicators.

WHY DEVELOP IMPROVED INDICATORS OF STUDENT COURSEWORK?

The need for improved coursework indicators can be substantiated on both educational research and policy grounds, and arguments for their development are reinforced by the limits of existing indicators.

The Link Between Coursework and Student Achievement

Research studies over the past fifteen years have documented the empirical relationship between student achievement, the types of courses taken, and the content and level of those courses. Raizen and Jones (1985) summarized four studies based on nationally representative student samples that showed a strong correlation between the number of mathematics courses students take and their achievement in mathematics. This relationship persists even when background variables such as home and community environment and previous mathematics learning are taken into account. Research has also shown that the level, as well as the number, of courses students take is correlated with achievement. Jones et al. (1986), after controlling for socioeconomic status (SES) and test scores two years earlier, found that students in the High School and Beyond (HS&B) sample with at least five transcript credits in mathematics courses at or above the algebra I level scored an average of 17 percentage points higher on a standardized mathematics test than those with no course credits in higher-level mathematics.

Some of the most compelling evidence about the relationship between achievement and curricular content comes from the Second International Mathematics Study (SIMS), which attempted to explain the poor performance of U.S. students relative to that of students in other industrialized countries. The SIMS researchers began by eliminating what they called "deceptive explanations." For example, they found that although the Japanese school year is longer than the U.S. school year (243 days vs. 180), Japanese students spend less time in mathematics instruction than their American counterparts (101 hours per year vs. 144). After eliminating the deceptive explanations, the researchers found real—and striking—differences between the ways curricula are organized in the highest-achieving countries and the way they are organized in the United States. At the lower-secondary level, the Japanese curriculum emphasizes algebra; the curricula in France and Belgium are dominated by geometry and fractions. In contrast, U.S. schools allocate their curricula more equally across a variety of topics—thus covering each subject much more superficially. The mathematics curriculum in U.S. schools is characterized by extensive repetition and review, and little intensity of coverage. This low-intensity coverage means that individual topics are treated in only a few class periods, and concepts and topics are quite fragmented (McKnight et al., 1987; Burstein, forthcoming).

Past research, most notably the SIMS, has produced two important findings for indicator development. First, research has shown that data on student test scores are of little use unless information is also available on the factors that influence the distribution of those scores across different types of students and schools and that help shape changes in achievement over time. Test-score data can indicate whether educational conditions are getting better or worse, but they provide little insight into why particular trends exist or how problems could be solved or successes replicated. For example, the most recent National Assessment of Educational Progress (NAEP) found that student gains in mathematics achievement since 1978 have been confined primarily to lower-order skills, and that only about half of all 17-year-olds have mastered mathematical procedures such as solving simple linear equations or making decisions based on information drawn from graphs (Dossey et al., 1988). That information, however, leaves some very basic questions unanswered: What kinds of students are most likely to lack these skills? Is the content on which students are being tested offered in most high school mathematics courses? Are the teachers who teach those courses adequately prepared to convey the relevant content?

... data on student test scores are of little use unless information is also available on the factors that influence the distribution of those scores across different types of students and schools and that help shape changes in achievement over time.

Indicator data on student outcomes document problems that need to be addressed; data on schooling trends, e.g., in coursework, help identify the sources of the problems and point to potential solutions.

... supplementing test-score data with information limited to course offerings and enrollments will not remedy the current inadequacies of most indicator systems.

The second important research finding is that supplementing test-score data with information limited to the titles of course offerings and enrollments will not remedy the current inadequacies of most indicator systems. Data on the types of courses that schools offer and the numbers of students enrolled in them provide only the most superficial understanding of the relationship between curriculum and achievement. As the SIMS results illustrate, the essential information is not just whether students take a particular course or even a sequence of courses, but rather what content is covered in those courses and how that content is presented. Measuring coursework solely by titles of offerings and numbers of enrollments produces confusing information that is of little use to either educational policy or instructional practice.

One of the major reasons for the lack of information conveyed by course titles alone is the differentiation of curricula within high schools according to student ability levels. Most comprehensive high schools have traditionally been characterized by multiple tracks, a system that has been shown to have clear consequences for the learning opportunities accorded different types of students (Oakes et al., 1990; Oakes, 1985; Gamoran and Berends, 1987; Gamoran, 1987). In some subject areas, particularly mathematics and science, such differences are partly captured in course titles or in the level designations appended to those titles. However, in other subject areas, such as social studies, course titles tell very little about the breadth or depth of content coverage or the instructional strategies used. The information problem is further confounded by the movement of some high schools away from tracking to heterogeneous classes while others maintain the traditional system.

Basing coursework measures on course titles will become even more problematic as curricular approaches change over the next decade. Professional groups such as the National Council of Teachers of Mathematics (NCTM) are recommending that mathematics courses and topics be reconfigured (e.g., they should more closely integrate ideas from algebra and geometry) as a way of strengthening high school mathematics instruction (NCTM, 1989). At the same time, some schools and districts have lengthened the traditional year-long algebra I sequence to two years to provide lower-achieving students with exposure to algebra. In a state where either of the above policies has been implemented, the titles of course offerings and enrollments will provide little information that is comparable over time or place.

Past research provides clear evidence to support the argument that indicator systems must include measures of student coursework. Research findings, coupled with the changing nature of curricula, also suggest that coursework indicators must be more sophisticated than simple counts of offerings and enrollments.

The Policy Community's Demand for Better Coursework Indicators

The call for improved indicators of student coursework is based not only on educational research, but also on the information needs of policymakers. More than at any other time in recent history, policymakers at all governmental levels are asking questions about public schools and taking actions that require more and better data. This interest in improved indicators is reflected at the federal level in efforts to expand and enhance the quality of national and international data; at the state level, in the work of organizations such as the Council of Chief State School Officers (CCSSO) to strengthen the capacity of states to collect and report indicator data and to standardize selected information across states; and at the district level, in the activities of individual states and local districts to track schooling conditions and monitor the progress of their educational reforms.

... the growing demand for better coursework indicators stems from the central fact that over the past decade, elected officials have extended their traditional concern about how schools are governed and financed to include what schools teach, who teaches it, and in some cases, how it is taught.

The growing demand for better coursework indicators stems from the central fact that over the past decade, elected officials, especially at the state level, have extended their traditional concern about how schools are governed and financed to include what schools teach, who teaches it, and in some cases, how it is taught. Figure 1.1 depicts this expansion of the policy sphere. The upper circle represents that part of the educational system most open to policy influence, the area of how schools are financed, governed, and organized. The lower circle includes the core features of schooling that are more difficult for policy to influence directly (e.g., student characteristics, teaching quality, and instructional methods). However, many factors lie between these two realms (e.g., how teachers are trained, what content students are taught). These factors affect the classroom directly but are also open to policy influences and have been the major targets of recent reform initiatives. Elements of schooling for which only practitioners needed information in the past are now also the purview of policymakers.

Policymakers are not only interested in the coursework content that students are receiving, they have also expressed concern about the effects of recent coursework policies on low-achieving students and about whether reforms have generated any unintended consequences, such as reduced curricular offerings or increased dropout rates.[2] They find that current data, based on simple enrollment counts, are inadequate for answering their questions.

... both sets of requirements should lead indicator designers to take into account the broader schooling context in which curriculum is delivered to students; how curriculum differs in content and treatment for different students; and depth as well as breadth of coverage.

This growing interest in monitoring the courses that different types of students are taking and in assessing the impacts of recent coursework policies has led policymakers to demand information that is quite similar to what research suggests is important. Both sets of requirements should lead indicator designers to take into account the broader schooling context in which curriculum is delivered to students; how curriculum differs

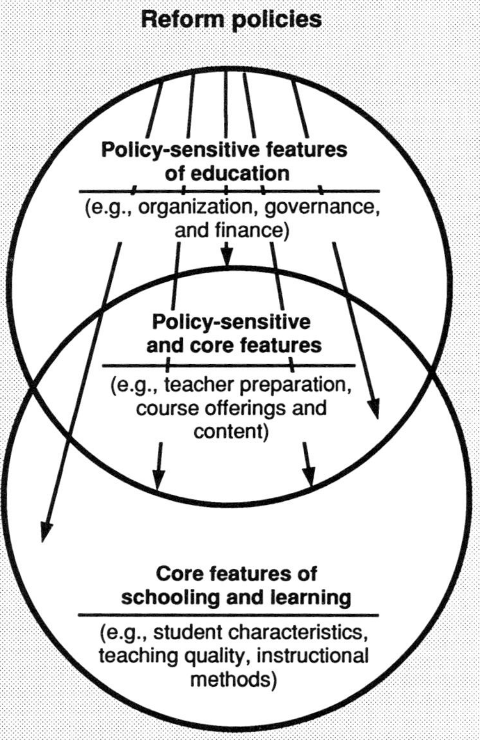

Fig. 1.1—The expansion of the educational policy system

---

[2]These information needs have been expressed by policymakers in various forums throughout the country; they also emerged in a focus group session that we conducted with 20 governors' education aides and in telephone interviews with staff from national associations representing state policymakers as well as state and local policymakers and their staffs.

in content and treatment for different students; and depth as well as breadth of coverage. With such data, the following kinds of policy questions could be answered more systematically:

- How do coursetaking patterns compare in urban and rural schools? Among students of different ethnic groups? Between boys and girls?
- Have state policies that increase course requirements for high school graduation resulted in students taking more difficult academic courses or just more lower-level ones?
- To what extent is the course content that is suggested (or mandated) by the state reflected in individual schools and classrooms?
- What is the match between teacher qualifications and their course assignments? In what courses are out-of-field assignments most prevalent?

The Limits of Existing Indicators

Even states with well-developed indicator systems, such as California, lack data beyond course enrollment statistics. More sophisticated indicator data are limited to national samples such as the National Education Longitudinal Study (NELS). California's school performance reports inform the public about enrollment trends in selected upper-level high school courses and the proportion of students enrolled in those courses required for admission to the University of California. However, they do not track trends in lower-level courses, nor do they provide information on whether course content is similar across schools or districts.

Several recent studies of trends in student coursetaking illustrate what can be learned from course enrollment data. These studies also indicate the limits of such information. A study conducted by Westat for the National Center for Education Statistics (NCES) compared the coursetaking patterns of 1987 high school graduates with those of students who completed high school in 1982. The data for the 1987 cohort were extracted from approximately 15,000 transcripts from a nationally representative sample of high schools selected for the 1985-86 NAEP and from 12,000 transcripts of 1982 high school graduates who participated in the HS&B study. Westat found that 77 percent of the class of 1987 had taken algebra I, as compared with 65 percent of the earlier cohort; the proportion of students taking biology had increased from 75 percent to 90 percent; and 71 percent of the 1987 graduates had taken at least one semester of American government, compared with 57 percent of the class of 1982 (Bennett, 1988). Other analyses of these same data compared rates of coursetaking by ethnicity, gender, and curricular track[3] (Goertz, 1989).

These studies provide evidence that coursetaking patterns in the immediate post-*Nation at Risk* period were consistent with policymakers' expectations in raising course requirements for high school graduation. They also provide some information on coursetaking patterns across different types of students—e.g., they reveal that the gap between the proportions of white and black students taking algebra is closing about three times as fast as the gap in geometry (Goertz, 1989: Table 10).

But there are many important questions that such data cannot answer. For example, they do not indicate whether the algebra I taken by the later cohort is essentially the same course as that offered to the earlier group. This is a significant issue because some qualitative data (e.g., Bureau of Research and Assessment, 1986) indicate that as more lower-ability students have been placed in algebra classes, teachers have had to cover fewer topics or cover them in less depth. However, other evidence suggests that the algebra I course may have become more rigorous as states and local school districts have moved to upgrade course quality through curriculum reform and textbook adoption policies. The data also reveal nothing about the relationship between Westat's classification of students into curricular tracks and their actual track assignments and exposure to subject-matter content within their own schools. This measure of curricular differentiation may also have little meaning over time as more schools move toward heterogeneous classes.

Other studies have examined trends in coursetaking on the basis of enrollment statistics. Hanson (1989) used data collected by the Florida Department of Education to analyze changes in coursetaking in 16 of the 24 secondary schools in Dade County. These data provide information on the number of sections of various courses that each school offers and the enrollment in those courses. Although such data do not provide student-level information, as transcript data do, they can indicate the distribution of enrollment within and across subject areas as coursetaking patterns shift. For example, Hanson found that mathematics enrollments had generally shifted toward less academically oriented courses (from algebra and computer applications to basic skills, informal geometry, and general mathematics). Across subject areas, science and foreign lan-

[3]Westat classified students in the academic track if they earned at least 12 credits in the core areas of English, history and social studies, mathematics, and/or science and did not meet the requirements for the vocational track. Students who earned at least 3 credits in an occupationally specific vocational education area and did not meet the requirements for the academic track were classified in the vocational track. Students who did not meet the requirements for either the academic or vocational track were classified as being in neither. This classification system is independent of the assignment policies of individual schools and has no direct relationship to the content of the courses students took.

guages gained largely at the expense of vocational education, which lost 19,000 students, or 65 percent of the enrollment increases experienced by other departments. This information is undoubtedly very important in tracking policy effects, but key pieces of data are missing.

Efforts are now being made to expand coursework indicators to include measures of course content and instructional strategies. However, such data are currently collected only on national samples and have not been incorporated into statewide indicator systems. In its teacher questionnaire, the NELS asks teachers of each student in the survey to report on the topics covered in their classes and the emphasis accorded each topic, and on the materials and types of instructional activities used.

Information is also requested about the ability level of each class. This information can relate course content to particular levels or tracks of the curriculum, yet it tells little about the curriculum offered students across the country. The NELS includes no questions about the amount of class time spent covering different topics, and no attempt is being made to validate the survey data with other data collection techniques that probe more deeply into the actual process of classroom instruction.

In arguing that coursework indicators need to measure more than course offerings and enrollments, we recognize that we are proposing that states expand their data collection efforts considerably. For example, according to Blank and Schilder (1989), only 29 states report mathematics and science enrollments by course, and only 23 report on the proportion of teachers teaching out-of-field, as defined by the teachers' certification status. Although a number of state education agencies indicated that they were considering collecting data on school- and classroom-level curriculum implementation (including reviews of school curriculum outlines, teacher surveys, classroom observations, and "opportunity-to-learn" or topic-coverage questionnaires), these were viewed as "potential" rather than actual methods of data collection (Blank, 1988). Nevertheless, the imperatives of policy and practice continue to move states toward designing and using more complete indicators of student coursework.

The next section outlines standards of technical validity and policy usefulness that should guide the design of coursework indicators.

2. DESIGN STANDARDS FOR COURSEWORK INDICATORS

Educational indicators must meet technical criteria that ensure validity, and they must be policy-relevant, useful, and feasible. This section outlines the design standards for coursework indicators. More general discussion of educational indicators can be found in Oakes (1986), OERI State Accountability Study Group (1988), and Shavelson et al. (1989).

VALID COURSEWORK INDICATORS

Indicators that validly measure which courses schools offer, the content included in those courses, and who teaches and enrolls in them should meet four technical criteria:

- They should be linked to a larger model of the schooling process.
- They should differentiate among tracks or levels of the curriculum.
- They should distinguish between the curriculum intended by designers and policymakers and the one actually implemented in schools and classrooms.
- To the extent possible, they should measure the depth of the curriculum as well as its breadth.

Embed Coursework Indicators in a Model of Schooling

Coursework indicators cannot be developed and used independently of indicators that measure the level and type of resources available to schools, the quality of the teaching staff, and a variety of student-related measures such as promotion and dropout rates, postsecondary matriculation, and a broad range of achievement scores. These indicators need to be interpreted within the context of a conceptual model of the ways different components of the educational system relate to one another. Without such a model, single indicators can easily be misinterpreted. The model may be simple and intuitive, or it can be more complex. The important point is that it should identify the major elements of the educational system and illustrate the relationships among those elements. Such a model cannot specify relationships in either a strictly predictive or a causal sense, but it can serve as a framework, showing logical linkages among parts of the schooling system and correlational relationships supported by past research. An understanding of these relationships is particularly important in interpreting trends in coursework indicators, e.g., how changes in coursetaking patterns or content coverage relate to demographic trends in school enrollments or to shifts in achievement test scores.

Differentiate Among Curricular Tracks or Levels

Indicators that attempt to describe curriculum without considering distinctions among student ability levels will obscure crucial attributes of the system, such as which students have access to what types of learning throughout their academic careers. We have already discussed the importance of measuring the extent to which curriculum is differentiated by student ability groupings. In some cases, those distinctions are clear from the course titles, but in many others, differences across levels are evident only if topic coverage and instructional strategies are examined.

Distinguish Between Intended and Implemented Curriculum

Curriculum can be defined in several ways, from the ideal standards rendered by subject-matter experts, to various state and local policies, to district curriculum guides, to teacher plans, to actual teacher-student interactions within classrooms (Oakes and Carey, 1989). Coursework indicators should characterize the implemented curriculum so that it can be compared with the intended one (Murnane and Raizen, 1988). Valid measures of the curriculum as it is actually presented in classrooms are needed to answer some very basic questions, e.g., What proportion of high school courses meet or exceed the curricular standards advocated by professional organizations in science, mathematics, or English? To what extent are state model curriculum frameworks reflected in teachers' content coverage and instructional strategies?

Measure the Breadth and Depth of the Curriculum

One solution to the problem of course titles providing inadequate information would be to measure the breadth of curricular content by determining what topics are covered in a particular course and the amount of time spent on each. However, as will be illustrated in Section 4, topic coverage in some subjects does not adequately distinguish among courses. For example, a basic or remedial-level U.S. history course might devote as much time to the Civil War as an advanced or honors-level course. What differentiates the two is the depth of coverage and the method of presentation. One course might stress discrete facts such as the dates of important battles, and might rely heavily on classroom lectures and on reading a textbook in class, while another class might focus on the broad social and economic issues raised by the Civil War and emphasize class discussions and independent student research. The depth of the curriculum needs to be measured if states and local districts are to have a robust set of coursework indicators.

POLICY-RELEVANT COURSEWORK INDICATORS

If coursework indicators are to inform policy and practice, they should meet more than technical standards—they should also contribute to policy decisions, and they should be feasible to collect and report.

Create Useful Coursework Indicators

Coursework indicators should be sensitive to major policy changes and they should provide information on the factors over which policy has some direct influence.

Indicator data do not afford the level of detail and rigor needed for careful evaluation of individual policies or programs (MacRae, 1985; Shavelson et al., 1989). However, such data can suggest whether trends in the status of key educational indicators are consistent with what policymakers hoped to achieve with particular types of policy. For example, policymakers may have expected higher graduation requirements to increase both the amount and academic rigor of high school coursetaking; a comprehensive set of coursework indicators could indicate whether or not such changes had occurred but could not be used to ascertain whether those changes were due to specific policy interventions or to other factors. In other words, indicator data cannot measure the independent effects of single policies, but they can signal whether changes are consistent with broad policy initiatives.

As the scope of educational policymaking continues to expand beyond the traditional focus on how schools are financed and governed to concerns about what is taught and who teaches it, indicator data that can inform policy decisions will become an increasingly essential resource. However, because of the immediacy of the policy community's information demands, some data that would be useful to educators and researchers may have low priority. A major criterion for the inclusion of any particular coursework indicator in a policy-relevant system will be its ability to measure a factor over which policymakers have some direct influence. For example, while the curricular goals that teachers seek to promote or the nature of their interactions with individual students are important to a valid understanding of the schooling process, these factors are far from the direct reach of policy. Therefore, when choices have to be made about which indicators to include in a state or local system, the highest priority should be given to those that measure factors most directly influenced by policy.

Emphasizing the information needs of policymakers and other nonexperts, however, does not preclude obtaining information that can also be useful to educators and researchers. The most effective indicators are those that serve multiple purposes. Section 4 presents an example of how the same indicator can be reported in different formats and levels of detail to accommodate different audiences. However, not all indicators are equally useful to all audiences, and a single indicator system may not meet the diverse information needs of policymakers, educators, the general public, parents, and researchers. While informing all these audiences should be a goal of indicator design, resource and other constraints may preclude its achievement. Therefore, indicators with explicit policy relevance should be given priority over factors less directly influenced by policy: Satisfying the information demands of policymakers is a primary function of indicator systems (McDonnell, 1989), and indicator data are not an efficient source of more idiosyncratic information about individual schools, classrooms, or students.

Design Indicators That Are Feasible to Collect and Use

The standards of technical validity and policy usefulness outlined above are ideals, and they must be tempered by the realities of policy and practice. Some of these realities relate to cost—for example, measuring curricular depth may require data collection methods that are too costly for widespread use by states and local districts. Some realities relate to the burden that can reasonably be imposed on schools for collecting indicator data and on state agencies for analyzing and interpreting them. Other constraints include the need to produce timely data on a schedule that is compatible with policymakers' decision cycles, and to report indicators that can be understood by a broad range of audiences—parents, policymakers, and newspaper readers, as well as educators.

Throughout the remainder of this guide, as we present sample coursework indicators and assess different strategies for collecting data on student coursework, we shall note the tradeoffs in cost and burden between less precise or less valid indicators and more sophisticated ones. First, however, we briefly summarize the research project from which they are derived.

3. THE SCHOOL REFORM ASSESSMENT PROJECT

The School Reform Assessment (SRA) project, a two-year exploratory design study, had two goals: to expand upon and refine the technical quality of existing coursework indicators, and to accommodate the information needs of policymakers by providing indicators that would measure, at least in a general way, the effects of major curriculum policies.

PURPOSE AND APPROACH

These two objectives narrowed our task to designing measures of coursetaking that could be implemented by state governments as part of their existing information gathering and indicator systems. We viewed our role as that of developing a template that states could adapt, after more extensive field-testing, to their own policy concerns, information needs, and data collection procedures. Thus, we had to concentrate on measures for which data could be efficiently collected through surveys of school administrators, teachers, and students.

... the major contribution of the SRA project would not be in developing entirely new indicators, but in refining existing indicators, adapting them to the framework of state indicator systems, and validating them through a number of benchmarking procedures.

We decided to draw primarily upon existing measures from sources such as the SIMS-IEA study, NELS, and NAEP. However, because the validity of many questionnaire items typically used in such studies has not been tested, we also undertook several benchmarking procedures, including interviews with school- and district-level personnel, evaluations of course materials, and the examination of student transcripts to verify data obtained from the surveys.[1] The in-depth interviews and course materials provide information that is much closer to the actual content of instruction than that provided by enrollment statistics or even most survey items; thus, they constitute evidence about validity or the extent to which more routinely collected data are accurately tapping what schools really teach.[2] Transcript analysis is an important source of historical data on how coursework patterns for different types of students have changed since the pre-reform period, and it provides a way of ascertaining whether the indicators we developed would be valid if the nature of the curriculum were to change significantly. Thus, we decided that the major contribution of the SRA project would not be in developing entirely new indicators, but in refining existing indicators, adapting them to the framework of state indicator systems, and validating them through a number of benchmarking procedures.

Because of resource and time constraints, we focused on three mathematics course categories—mathematics below algebra I (e.g., general mathematics, consumer mathematics, pre-algebra), algebra I, and algebra II—

[1]The role of benchmark data in a state indicator system is discussed at length in Section 5.

[2]Forthcoming report by Daniel Koretz, The RAND Corporation.

and two social studies courses—U.S. history and U.S. government. These subjects were selected because they were particularly affected by changes in state high school graduation requirements. The specific course categories were chosen because analyses of local responses to state curriculum policies suggested that these categories would capture the range of local effects (Clune, White, and Patterson, 1989). Although this development effort is limited to five course categories, we believe that it can serve as a prototype for other subjects and courses.

THE STUDY SAMPLE AND ITS LIMITATIONS

This study was conducted in two states, California and Georgia, to control for the policy context in which indicators would be developed and used. By taking into account state policies, we could develop indicators that would be useful for assessing how the coursework delivered in local high schools compares with state curricular objectives. These two states were selected because data on their recent policies and local responses to those policies were available from earlier research.

As noted in Section 1, California's indicator system is one of the most highly developed state systems in the country, but its information on student coursetaking is limited to school-level enrollment statistics collected by course title. Because California has engaged in a major effort to upgrade its state-developed curriculum frameworks, it is particularly important that new indicators measure the extent to which the content of those frameworks is reflected in school- and classroom-level curricula.

Georgia is currently developing a more comprehensive state indicator system, including a new course categorization system. An approach like the one used in the SRA study could help to answer a practical question that state officials have asked: Can Georgia use a single designation for a course such as algebra I, or will it need multiple designations to distinguish among very different levels and content? The Georgia system offers three different diplomas—general, college preparatory, and vocational—each with different coursework requirements, and this affords an additional basis for measuring curricular differentiation.[3]

[3]Both California and Georgia also increased course requirements for high school graduation in the 1980s. California requires 22 Carnegie units, including 13 in particular courses: three years of English, two of mathematics, two of science, three of social studies (including U.S. and world history and culture, economics, geography, and U.S. government), one of fine arts or foreign language, and two of physical education. These requirements became effective with the graduating class of 1987.

Georgia requires 21 units, of which 13 are specified by the state: four years of English, two of mathematics, two of science, three of social studies, one of physical education, and one of computer technology, fine arts, or vocational education. The course requirements became effective with the class of 1988.

We used seven high schools as data sources for our validation study.[4] These schools do not in any way constitute a representative sample of high schools in California or Georgia. Our strategy of combining surveys with detailed benchmark data required us to limit our sample to a small number of schools; and several of those we contacted refused to participate.[5] Nevertheless, the participating schools do vary in location, size, ethnic composition, and extent of curricular differentiation.[6] The sample is described in greater detail in the Appendix.

Although the sample is small and not representative, it enabled us to develop a unique database for designing indicators that overcome the shortcomings of current measures. The data enable coursework to be assessed in greater depth than is possible with the type of statistics now used in most state indicator systems; they provide a greater span of variation than is possible in most ethnographic studies; and they allow for the evaluation of a variety of statistical measures that are often used in large national studies but rarely judged as to their validity.

DATA COLLECTION PROCEDURES

The five types of data collected in each school are summarized in Fig. 3.1. The teacher and student surveys are described below, and the remaining data are reviewed in Section 5.

Teacher Surveys

We assumed that these surveys would eventually be administered as part of the process of routine state data collection; therefore they were designed to take teachers only about 30 minutes to complete. In every school, all of the teachers who taught any mathematics or social studies course in the 1987-88 academic year were surveyed. They were first asked questions about their educational background (e.g., number of mathematics or social studies courses taken, amount of subject-matter inservice over the past three years) and experience. They were then asked

---

[4]Five of the schools included grades 9–12; two of the Georgia schools contained only grades 10–12. For the latter two schools, ninth-grade mathematics and social studies teachers were surveyed at the junior high schools that served as feeder schools.

[5]Despite the problems that we experienced in gaining access to high schools, we decided not to reduce the scope of our data collection (e.g., by eliminating the transcript analysis or limiting the number of students surveyed). Had we done that, access would not have been a problem, but the quality of our validation effort would have been severely compromised. We also felt that since state governments would be the agencies most likely to field-test our indicators in the future, their authority to mandate such data collection would mean that the indicators would eventually be field-tested on an entire population or a representative sample of high schools.

[6]Five of the seven schools have a majority Anglo enrollment (55 to 65 percent); one has a majority of Hispanics; and the other has an enrollment almost equally divided among Anglos, Blacks, and Hispanics. The proportion of students going on to attend four-year colleges ranges from 7 to 28 percent across the seven schools. Three schools have a minimal amount of formal differentiation among levels of the curriculum, with only regular and honors classes offered; three are highly differentiated, offering up to four different levels; and one is moderately differentiated, with remedial, regular, and honors classes in some subjects, but only regular and honors classes in others.

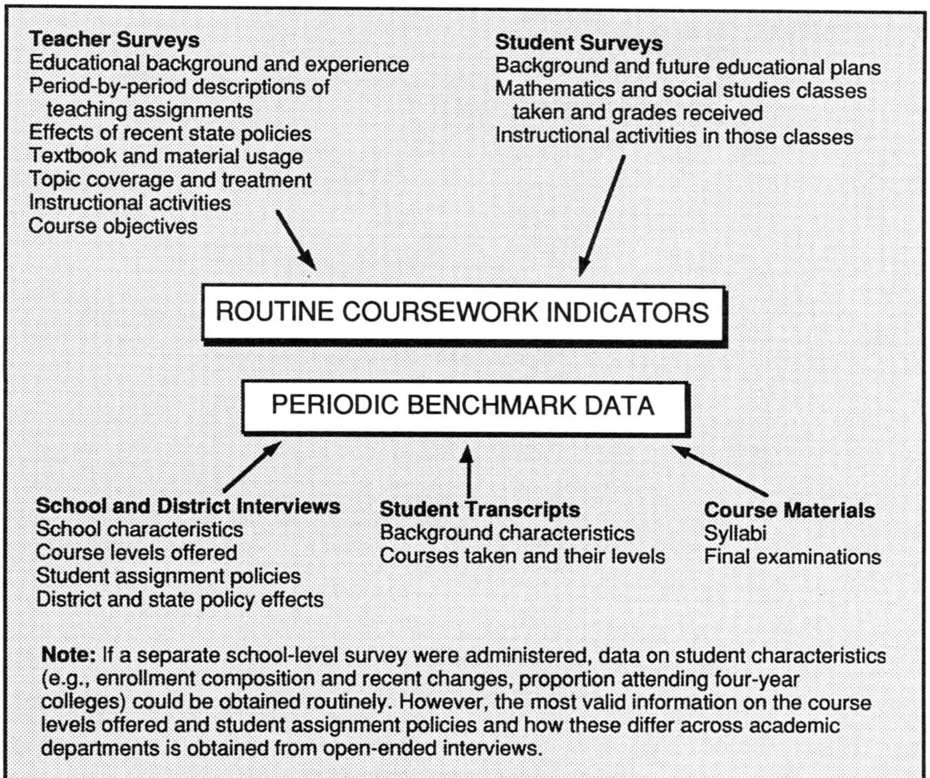

Teacher Surveys
Educational background and experience
Period-by-period descriptions of teaching assignments
Effects of recent state policies
Textbook and material usage
Topic coverage and treatment
Instructional activities
Course objectives
Student Surveys
Background and future educational plans
Mathematics and social studies classes taken and grades received
Instructional activities in those classes
ROUTINE COURSEWORK INDICATORS
PERIODIC BENCHMARK DATA
School and District Interviews
School characteristics
Course levels offered
Student assignment policies
District and state policy effects
Student Transcripts
Background characteristics
Courses taken and their levels
Course Materials
Syllabi
Final examinations
Note: If a separate school-level survey were administered, data on student characteristics (e.g., enrollment composition and recent changes, proportion attending four-year colleges) could be obtained routinely. However, the most valid information on the course levels offered and student assignment policies and how these differ across academic departments is obtained from open-ended interviews.

Fig. 3.1—SRA data sources

to give a period-by-period description of the classes they taught (including those outside mathematics and social studies), to provide some information about teacher assignment patterns, and to indicate whether and in what ways any of these courses may have been affected by recent changes in state graduation requirements or other state policies.

Those teachers who taught any of the five courses being considered in the SRA were then asked to complete a separate survey (still included in the 30-minute time limit) for each section of a course that they taught in a significantly different way.[7] Teachers were asked about textbooks and

---

[7]Respondents who taught multiple sections of the same course to students at the same ability level using the same instructional strategies were asked to complete only one form. Therefore, the number of sections listed in the Appendix is lower than the total number offered across the seven schools.

If teachers taught more than two sections with significantly different content and instructional approaches, they needed about 45 minutes to complete the survey.

other materials; topic coverage;[8] the number of periods devoted to each topic; and whether the topic was taught as new content, reviewed and extended, reviewed only, assumed as prerequisite knowledge, or not taught and not assumed as student knowledge (essentially the SIMS-IEA strategy for ascertaining depth of coverage). Respondents were also asked about their instructional strategies (an adaptation of the NAEP, IEA, and NELS items),[9] their goals for the course, the types of assignments and examinations they gave, their distribution of grades, student preparation, and level of student performance, given that preparation.

Student Surveys

Our student surveys were designed as questionnaires that states could administer in conjunction with their standardized achievement tests. Consequently, these surveys were even shorter than those administered to teachers: Surveys for tenth graders required approximately 10 minutes, those for twelfth graders, 15 to 20 minutes. They were administered to all tenth and twelfth graders in attendance on a particular day. The surveys included items about each student's background and future educational plans, as well as questions that repeated the instructional strategy items asked of teachers. In this way, the students could be linked to individual teachers, and the level of agreement between the two data sources could be evaluated.

HOW THE SRA FINDINGS ARE USED IN THIS REPORT

Because this report is designed as a policy guide, SRA project results are used here only as examples to illustrate the range of coursework indicators that states might consider adopting and the relative merits of different strategies for collecting data on those indicators.[10]

The goal of the SRA project was to aid in the development, rather than the production, of coursework indicators. Therefore, sample size and statistical representativeness were less important than capturing the range of variability in coursework conditions and assessing the accuracy

---

[8]The mathematics topics included in the survey (15 for algebra II and 23 for the other mathematics courses) are similar to those used in the SIMS-IEA study and the Center for Research on Evaluation, Standards, and Student Testing (CRESST) Instructional Assessment Project. Fifteen U.S. history and government topics were selected for each course; these included historical events, political institutions, and concepts (e.g., the potential conflict between liberty and equality). We based our choices on curriculum frameworks such as those in California and consultations with historians and political scientists.

[9]Mathematics teachers were given questions about 14 different instructional strategies (e.g., the review of homework problems in class, small group work, the use of calculators and computers) and the frequency with which they were used. History and government teachers were given questions about 12 instructional strategies (e.g., lecturing to the class, student presentations, reading primary materials) and the frequency of their use.

[10]A complete summary of study findings and a discussion of the technical issues involved in designing coursework indicators are included in *The Design of Improved Coursework Indicators: First Steps,* available from the Center for Research on Evaluation, Standards, and Student Testing, UCLA Graduate School of Education, Los Angeles, California.

with which different measures described those conditions. We collected more data than would be necessary for a routine indicator system and traded large sample size for depth of information. As a result, issues of statistical significance were of less importance in reporting findings than simulating the reasoning one would apply in using indicator data to evaluate student coursework. Measures of statistical significance are not reported in the examples discussed here, although for some analyses, they were used heuristically. The project findings should not be interpreted as representative of the effects of coursework reforms in California or Georgia, nor do the examples illustrate all of the information that coursework indicators can convey.

The next section depicts sample coursework indicators developed in the SRA and describes the kinds of information that each measure generates. Section 5 uses study findings as a basis for assessing alternative data collection strategies.

4. SAMPLE COURSEWORK INDICATORS

The basic elements of student coursework considered here are content or topic coverage, instructional strategies, curricular objectives, and teacher qualifications. Schools' performance on each of these dimensions can be gauged in a variety of ways. This section presents indicators to measure each element and illustrates how they can be used separately and together to document what schools are teaching.

TOPIC COVERAGE

The number of periods teachers devote to a topic and the way they treat that topic in a particular section constitute a workable indicator that states might use to measure coursework patterns and trends. Six alternative topic coverage indicators and their major shortcomings are listed below:

- *Course offerings and enrollment based on generic titles.* These data do not indicate the variability in material covered in courses with the same title (see Section 1).
- *Textbook use.* This measure is imprecise because it does not tell which parts of the text are actually covered in a particular class or how teachers may supplement textbooks with additional material. Breadth and depth of coverage can be measured only through a time-consuming process of mapping textbook content with what is taught in the classroom.
- *Textbook plus chapters covered.* This measure reduces the problem of inferences about coverage based on knowing only which textbook is used, but some mapping is still required.
- *Syllabus or syllabus plus class assignments, exercises, and examinations.* This measure, while more valid than the previous three, still requires considerable effort to ensure that it is interpreted correctly. Inclusion on a syllabus provides no information about how a topic was treated from the teacher's perspective;[1] assignment and examination analysis depends on the comprehensiveness and representativeness of the material provided, and considerable effort may also be required to derive measures of topic coverage and treatment (i.e., the

---

[1]The syllabus as a measure of topic coverage and treatment within individual classrooms may become an even less valid indicator as schools and districts seek greater standardization of their courses. For example, in several schools in the SRA sample, teachers used a department-wide syllabus that was common to all sections of a course taught within that school. However, our survey data indicate that despite this common syllabus, topic coverage varied across sections of the same course. One urban school in our sample used district-wide syllabi, and variation again occurred across sections.

breadth and depth of the curriculum as it is actually presented in the classroom).

- *Opportunity-to-learn (OTL), as measured by test items.* Under this approach, used in the SIMS study, teachers are asked whether their students were taught the material necessary to answer specific test items; if they were not, why not; and what proportion of students in the class could answer each test item. The OTL measure requires teachers to respond to items from a curriculum achievement test. The SIMS researchers found that teachers may respond to the wrong characteristics of some items or may overlook the fact that an item taps multiple dimensions. For example, mathematics items that deal with the concept of similar triangles may be embedded in word problems or graphical representations, but teachers may focus on the concept itself and not on whether students were taught to apply that concept in different formats.
- *Ongoing, detailed classroom observations.* This is the best way to make valid inferences about the curriculum that students are actually receiving. However, classroom observation is not feasible for a statewide indicator system because it is time-consuming and labor-intensive. Standardization requires well-trained, experienced observers, and extensive observation is necessary to monitor topics as they are introduced and then later reviewed and expanded or extended.

Topic coverage, in terms of time and treatment, is a middle-range indicator that balances fidelity to coursework coverage and emphasis with respondent burden and cost.[2] Other ways of gaining in-depth descriptions of the curriculum have greater validity, but most means of obtaining such information on a large scale are either more crude (e.g, they represent the intended rather than the implemented curriculum) or more costly in terms of personnel, time, and resources.

Topic Coverage Indicators and the Information They Provide

Topic coverage indicators can be used in several ways to provide data about coursework patterns. The discussion below describes some of these ways. Problems that may be encountered in operationalizing topic coverage indicators are also discussed.

---

[2]The SRA survey, administered in fall 1988, asked teachers about the number of periods they devoted to specific topics and the treatment they gave them during the previous academic year. While this approach may have sacrificed some accuracy, since it depends on teachers' ability to recall what they had taught over the preceding twelve months, it allowed them to describe an entire course, based on their actual teaching rather than on their plans for upcoming classes. Data of this kind might be more reliable if they were collected in late May or early June for the current academic year.

Average topic coverage in U.S. history and government. Figure 4.1 and Table 4.1 show the average number of periods that U.S. history and government teachers reported spending on different topics. These are examples of the simplest uses of topic coverage indicators, but they convey some important information. For example, Fig. 4.1 shows that with the exception of westward and overseas expansion, on which the Georgia schools spent an average of two weeks more than the California schools, the sample schools in the two states averaged about the same amount of time on each topic. However, as shown in Table 4.1, there was considerable variation among sections in the number of periods spent on a particular topic. This variation occurred not just across the entire sample, but also within a given school. For example, in the suburban Georgia school, some teachers reported having spent only a week on the Constitution, while others spent two weeks; some spent less than a week each on the scope and limits of presidential power and on major social issues, while others spent more than two weeks on those topics. Given that U.S. government is a one-semester course, a difference of one week changes the course emphasis considerably. In U.S. history, the amount of time spent on a particular topic differed by as much as three weeks

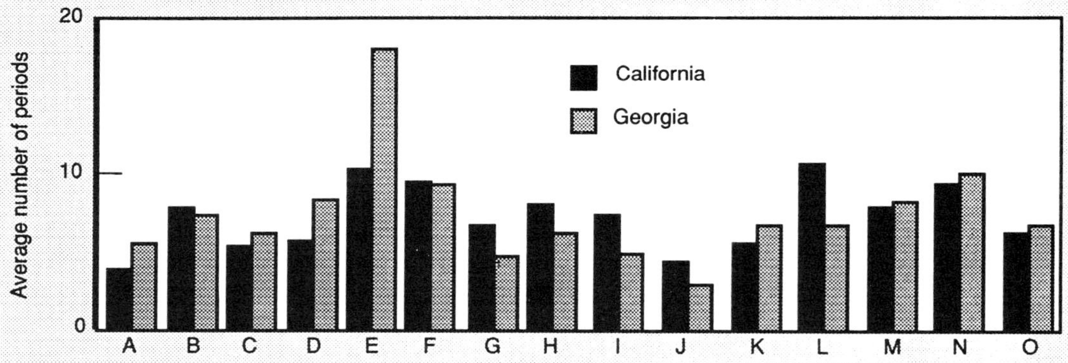

A. Age of exploration
B. Colonial America
C. Ideological origins of American revolution
D. Framing the Constitution
E. Westward/overseas expansion
F. Civil War
G. Reconstruction
H. Growth of U.S. as an industrial power
I. Progressive era
J. Immigration
K. World War I
L. Great Depression/New Deal
M. World War II
N. Cold War
O. Civil Rights

Fig. 4.1—Periods spent on selected history topics, by state

Table 4.1

PERIODS SPENT ON U.S. GOVERNMENT TOPICS IN HIGH SCHOOL HISTORY CLASSES

Topic	Average No. of Periods	Range
U.S. Constitution and Bill of Rights	8.7	2–20
Due process	3.5	1–10
Potential conflict between liberty and equality	2.8	0–7
Federalist paper #51	0.5	0–2
Congress	9.8	2–15
Role of interest groups	2.4	0–5
Scope and limits of presidential power	5.9	2–15
Court system	8.2	2–20
Major Supreme Court decisions	3.4	0–10
Political parties, elections, and voting	6.9	2–15
State and local government	5.1	0–15
Different forms of government outside the United States	4.0	0–20
Major social issues	5.3	2–12
Rights and responsibilities of citizens	5.0	1–12

among classes within the same school. The most significant variation occurred in analytical topics, such as the ideological origins of the American revolution, and in topics from recent history, such as the civil rights movement and the cold war.

Uses of average topic coverage information. Although the topics in the SRA instruments were selected to be neutral with regard to either curricular preferences or specific policies, the information generated from topic coverage indicators can be used to compare coursework patterns against a variety of standards. For example, it has been argued that the time a teacher spends on a particular topic is largely determined by the amount of coverage the textbook devotes to that topic. We performed a limited analysis to test the validity of that argument. We examined four of the thirteen U.S. history texts used by teachers in the SRA sample and calculated the number of pages devoted to each topic as a proportion of the pages devoted to the fifteen topics listed on the survey. We then compared this with the number of periods teachers reported spending on each topic as a proportion of the total number of reported periods. We found that the correlation between textbook and teacher coverage across all the history topics was 0.5; however, no consistent pattern emerged. For some topics, teachers followed the relative emphasis of the textbook exactly; for others, they devoted considerably more or less attention than did the textbook.

Topic coverage might also indicate whether curricular patterns have changed with policy actions. For example, the data on California schools might be viewed as a baseline. The relative emphasis accorded different U.S. history topics might be expected to shift as schools implement the state curriculum framework that concentrates eleventh grade U.S. history on the twentieth century. And in fact, teachers reported in their responses to open-ended questions that they were beginning to adapt to the new frameworks, for example, by moving quickly through earlier periods in order to be able to spend the entire second semester on the twentieth century. If data of the type collected in the SRA study were gathered regularly, this adaptation to new policy guidance could be expected to appear in the quantitative indicators over a period of several years.

The relative emphasis accorded different topics could also be used to assess the implemented curriculum according to different professional standards. For example, Table 4.1 presents a picture of U.S. government coursework that emphasizes public law and formal institutions (e.g., the Constitution and the court system) and pays considerably less attention to political dynamics and policy outputs (e.g., the conflict between liberty and equality, the role of interest groups, major Supreme Court decisions). Political scientists might argue that such a curricular approach portrays American government as more static than it actually is and that it minimizes the degree of conflict inherent in the political process. On the other hand, some educators might argue that since U.S. government is for many students the last formal exposure to the fundamentals of the American political system, a basic grounding in the legal structure of the system should be provided so that students can access the governmental services to which they are entitled and understand the terminology used in televised news reports. Thus, although indicators should be as neutral as possible, they should be designed to provide information that can be compared against a variety of standards.

The need for more extensive social-studies indicator development. Very little developmental work has been done on indicators of social studies coursework, in contrast to the amount of research that has been devoted to mathematics and science indicators. A few national studies, such as the NELS, have included history topics in their teacher surveys, but the topics tend to be limited to very general categories of historical events. In contrast, mathematics indicator development has drawn on extensive work undertaken as part of achievement test, curriculum, and indicator development efforts. The choice of social studies topics for the SRA project was based on an examination of curriculum frameworks and textbooks and on a desire to include both broad and narrow topics in history, and in government to include ones that spanned political institutions, policy processes, and more complicated analytical concepts. We believe that while our choice of topics has yielded valuable information, more extensive developmental work like that already completed in mathematics and science should be undertaken in social studies.[3]

Proportionate coverage of mathematics topics. How much of an academic subject's core content is covered in a typical class?[4] And does that proportion vary significantly across courses and sections? Coursework indicators can answer these questions, but they must be more sophisticated than just the average scores that are most commonly reported. Data from the SRA survey of teachers of algebra I and lower-level mathematics illustrate how coursework indicators can be used for such a purpose.

In developing indicators of coursework coverage in mathematics, the SRA project built on research begun during the SIMS study and extended as part of CRESST's cooperation with the Math Diagnostic Testing Program (MDTP), in which a cross-classification scheme for test items and curricular topics was designed and field-tested (see Burstein et al., 1986; Burstein, Chen, and Kim, 1989). The 23 topics included on the SRA survey of algebra I and lower-level mathematics courses were selected from the MDTP Teacher Topic Coverage Questionnaire. They are representative of the content covered in algebra I and lower-level courses; some are quite general, and others are more detailed. Table 4.2 lists the 23 topics, categorized into four broad groups.[5]

Figure 4.2 displays information about the distribution of topic coverage across sections in a more comprehensive way than is possible with simple numerical or graphical representations of the average number of pe-

---

[3]Differences between the level of sophistication of mathematics and science indicators and that of social studies and English indicators may be partly due to the nature of the two disciplines: mathematics and science consist of what is often perceived to be more hierarchically ordered knowledge, and they enjoy somewhat greater expert consensus about which content is central to the curriculum. However, the differing stages of indicator development are also the result of significantly greater investment in science and mathematics curriculum and indicator research, largely the result of funding by the National Science Foundation.

[4]"Core content" can be defined in a number of different ways. For example, some might think of it as curricular expectations about what knowledge and skills instruction ought to provide and would thus rely on pronouncements of groups such as the National Science Board and expert committees and on model curriculum frameworks for a definition. It might also be defined through a review of textbooks, district scope and sequence guides, or past research on what is actually taught in a given subject.

We have defined core mathematics content empirically rather than normatively, using past research on teachers' topic coverage. However, we have also considered expert opinions about what should be included in core content, as a basis for comparison.

[5]This set of topics is not intended to be exhaustive for any course. Other topics that might have been sampled include ratio, proportion, and percent; exponents; proportional reasoning; basic properties of triangles; and the Pythagorean theorem. Including all of these would have broadened the coverage of high-level arithmetic and pre-algebra core material. Perhaps a better balance might be struck, but we would be uncomfortable about expanding the list to ask teachers about more than 25 to 30 topics. While some adjustment may be needed in the balance among topics, we feel that the general strategy is sound.

Table 4.2

REPRESENTATIVE MATHEMATICS TOPICS COVERED IN ALGEBRA I AND LOWER-LEVEL COURSES

Arithmetic	*Pre-algebra*[a]
Arithmetic operations with whole numbers	Prime factorization
Common fractions (operations, evaluation, comparisons)	Square roots
Decimal fractions	Coordinate plane formulas (e.g., area, volume)
Conversions among fractions, decimals, percentages	
Algebra core[b]	*Enriched/advanced*[c]
Operations with radical and rational expressions	Solving quadratic equations
Operations with polynomials	Graphing equations and inequalities
Factoring	Probability
Solving linear equations	Statistics
Applications of equations	Applications of parallelism and perpendicularity
Generating algebraic equations from word problems	Function concept, use of function notation
Inequalities	Graphing of functions
Solutions of equations with absolute values	

[a]These topics are typically introduced in pre-algebra courses, although brief introductions to them are likely to occur in earlier courses.

[b]These topics are virtually universal in standard first-year algebra courses.

[c]These topics either have no fixed place in the curriculum (e.g., probability, descriptive statistics) or are typically covered at the end of algebra I but not emphasized until geometry or algebra II.

riods devoted to different topics (like those used to illustrate the SRA social studies data). The plots in Fig. 4.2 convey considerably more information about the distribution of topic coverage than do means and ranges. The line across the middle of each "box" represents the median; the lower and upper boundaries of the box equal the twenty-fifth and seventy-fifth percentiles; the "whiskers" depict the tenth and ninetieth percentiles; and the dots represent outliers beyond the tenth and ninetieth percentiles. The left-hand side of Fig. 4.2 combines the arithmetic and pre-algebra topics, and the right-hand side combines the algebra and enriched topics.

This example illustrates quite vividly that while students in a typical algebra I section were provided more exposure to algebra and enriched topics than their counterparts in either pre-algebra or general mathematics classes, the content coverage varied enormously across sections of courses with the same title. In the typical algebra I section, teachers reported covering 80 percent of the algebra and enriched topics, compared with 60 percent in the typical pre-algebra class and 27 percent in general

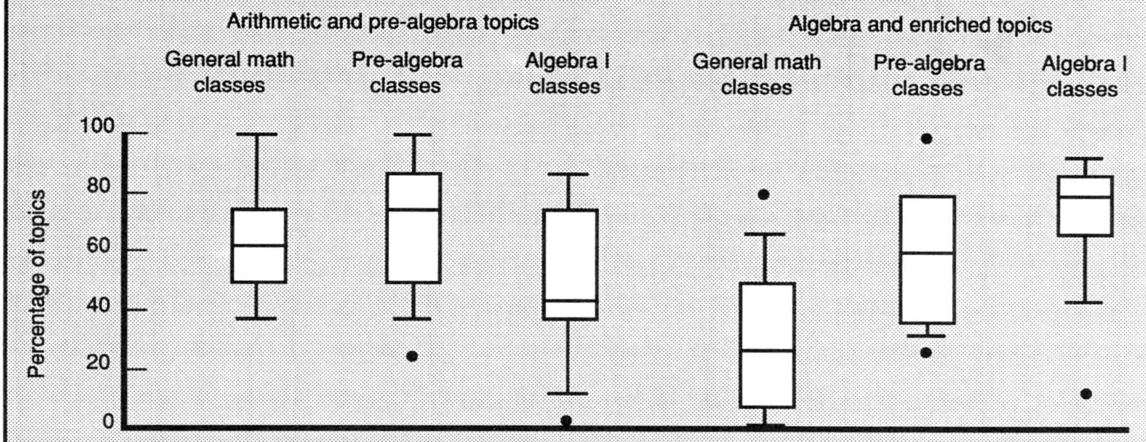

Fig. 4.2—Proportion of mathematics topics taught as new or reviewed and extended material, by class title

mathematics. However, the median scores mask considerable diversity within each course; some pre-algebra and general mathematics classes covered as much algebra and enriched topics as some algebra I classes, although the depth of coverage might have differed. Excluding the extreme values, the proportion of topics covered ranged from 44 to 93 percent in algebra I sections, and from 33 to 80 percent in pre-algebra. Teachers in a quarter of the pre-algebra sections reported covering at least as high a proportion of algebra and enriched topics as did the bottom half of the algebra I classes. The range of topic coverage was even greater across general mathematics sections, with the proportion varying from 0 to 67 percent.

... this example illustrates quite vividly that while students in a typical algebra I section were provided more exposure to algebra and enriched topics than their counterparts in either pre-algebra or general mathematics classes, the content coverage varied enormously across sections of courses with the same title.

The same finding holds for arithmetic and pre-algebra topics. Particularly striking is the amount of variation within algebra I: Although 44 percent of the arithmetic and pre-algebra topics were taught to the typical algebra I class as new or reviewed/extended material, the proportion of lower-level topics covered in algebra I ranged from 13 to 88 percent.

Material of the type represented by this example is more complicated and difficult to report than most indicator data—especially to diverse, nontechnical audiences. Yet it is precisely the kind of information needed by policymakers and educators who are concerned about curricular rigor and equitable learning opportunities. Such topic coverage indicators can provide different levels of detail for different audiences.

... topic coverage indicators can provide different levels of detail for different audiences.

For example, the most important, and also the most general, conclusion to be drawn from the data on topic coverage in mathematics is that because course titles mask considerable variability, some algebra I students are receiving no more exposure to algebra content than students enrolled in some general mathematics and pre-algebra classes. This is probably as much information as policymakers and top-level administrators need or want. On the other hand, state and local curriculum experts need more detail about the configurations of topics covered in different classes and the amount of attention and type of treatment given them. Not all indicators can serve multiple purposes, but wherever possible, system designers need to think about how to use the same indicator for reporting different types of information at different levels of detail to minimize the data collection burden.

INSTRUCTIONAL ACTIVITIES AND CLASS ASSIGNMENTS

A comprehensive picture of a curriculum requires information not only about the content covered, but also about the instructional strategies employed to convey that content. Key elements include the manner in which content is sequenced and the mode in which teachers and textbooks present it to students. For example, research has shown that if students are to learn to use science and mathematics as tools for dealing with real-world situations, they must be exposed to actual problems and not just routine exercises, and they need to learn how to apply a variety of organized approaches to problem solving. Thus, curriculum indicators "should provide information about the degree to which students experience the curriculum in a problem-solving mode rather than as exercises that are relatively straightforward translations of procedures" (Oakes and Carey, 1989: 110). However, such information (e.g., the number of problems presented in a class that are not direct applications of the textbook) is often too difficult or too burdensome to obtain in routine data collection.

Consequently, state indicator systems will have to rely on proxy measures that sacrifice some validity and comprehensiveness for the sake of feasibility. Information about the mode in which content is delivered to students can be obtained, for example, by asking about the frequency with which teachers use different instructional strategies. This approach has been used in several national and international studies, including NELS, NAEP, the 1985 National Survey of Science and Mathematics Education (NSSME), and the SIMS, and it is the approach that was used in the SRA project. Asking teachers about instructional activities and class assignments is a cost-efficient compromise between the status quo, where states have little or no information about how content is delivered to students, and a detailed (and costly) examination of instructional practices.

We used two criteria in selecting activities and assignments to include on the SRA survey. First, we wanted a balance between commonly used instructional techniques (e.g., lecturing, having students read the textbook in class) and activities associated with reform proposals to improve students' critical thinking skills (e.g., the use of hands-on materials or having students work in small groups, write research papers, and conduct special projects). Second, since one purpose of the SRA project was to assess alternative data collection strategies, we wanted to obtain information about classroom activities from both teachers and students. Consequently, we selected a set of activities and assignments and a metric for reporting their frequency that we believed could be understood by both teachers and students.[6] Where feasible, we included items from the major national studies.

Using Activities and Assignments to Characterize Classes of Different Ability Levels

Information about instructional strategies can be used in a variety of ways to portray the curriculum that different types of students are receiving. Figures 4.3 and 4.4 illustrate variation in activities and assignments by class ability level for homogeneously grouped U.S. history and government sections.[7]

The figures show significant contrasts across classes of different ability levels, but also several striking similarities. First, teachers lecture almost daily in the majority of classes at all levels. Second, the proportion of sections engaging in class discussion almost every day is the same for the low-ability classes as for the high-ability classes. This finding clearly illustrates the limitation of using numbers of activities and assignments as a measure. It is likely that the content of class discussions differs across the two levels, as do teachers' goals and expectations in using this instructional technique. However, such differences cannot be ascertained by measuring only frequency of activities.

---

[6]Section 5 assesses the relative merits of collecting coursework data from students and from teachers.

[7]Thirty-five of the 66 history and government sections in the SRA sample were, by teacher report, homogeneously grouped, with all students having the same ability level (either low, average, or high). The remaining 29 sections were reported by teachers to be heterogeneous, with a mixture of two or more ability levels. The profile of the mixed classes is most like that of the average-ability classes for all activities except lecturing and seatwork; the proportion of sections engaging in those activities almost every day is closer to that of the low-ability classes.

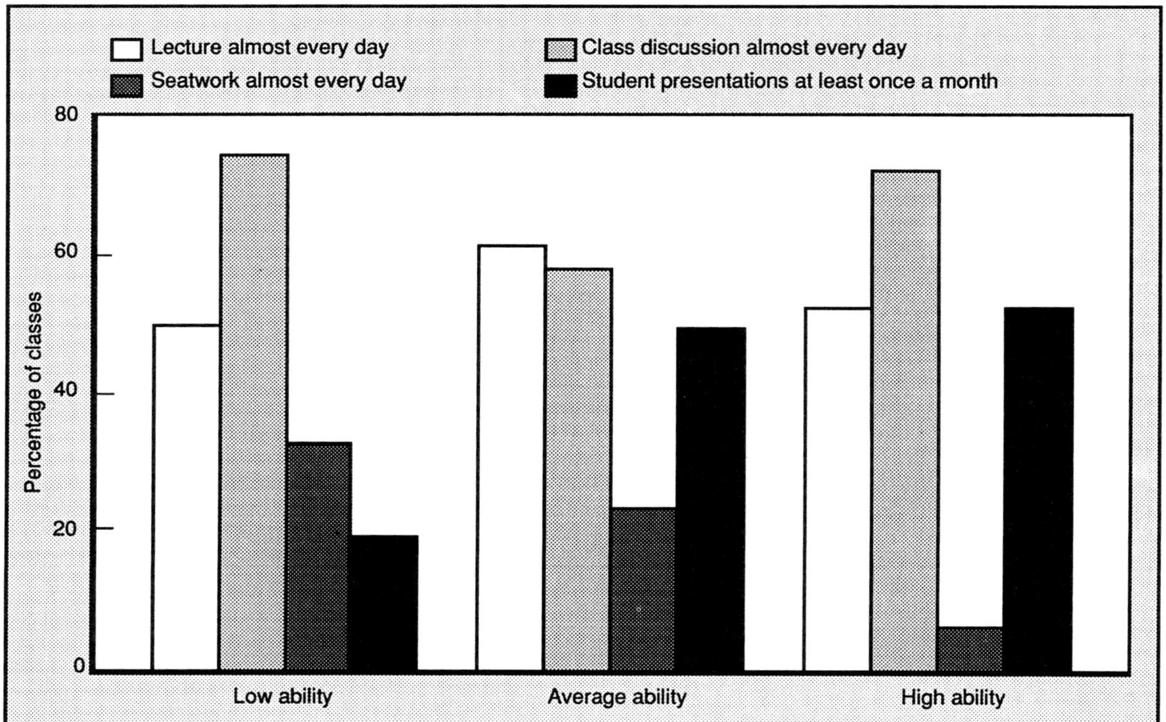

Fig. 4.3—Frequency of activities, by class ability

Differences across levels for the remaining activities and assignments are consistent with the research on curriculum stratification (see Gamoran and Berends, 1987). For example, considerably fewer high- than low-ability classes engage in seatwork almost every day; but more than twice as many high- and average-ability classes require student presentations monthly or more often. Reading primary materials and writing research papers are class assignments associated with teaching students problem-solving and critical-thinking skills. In the SRA sample, the high-ability classes are three times as likely as the low-ability ones to write research papers and twice as likely to read primary materials on a regular basis.

The Effectiveness of Different Measures for Characterizing Class Ability Levels

Evidence from the SRA study suggests that particular measures may characterize courses more validly in some subject areas than in others. For example, although instructional strategies were found to distinguish among ability levels in social studies, activities and assignments did not provide similar information for mathematics courses. The mathematics activities that occurred most frequently in the SRA sample—explaining a lesson to the entire class, reviewing homework problems, teachers working problems at the board, and students working on problems alone—were similar across courses and ability levels. The activities and assignments that occurred least often—the use of computers, students making oral reports, special projects, and mathematics labs—were also similar across mathematics courses of all levels. Topic coverage and treatment were more effective for distinguishing among class ability levels than instructional strategies. Nevertheless, the activity profile of mathematics classes that emerges in the SRA sample provides other important information—e.g., that teachers are relying primarily on a traditional set of activities and assignments which differ from the reform proposals of professional mathematics groups.

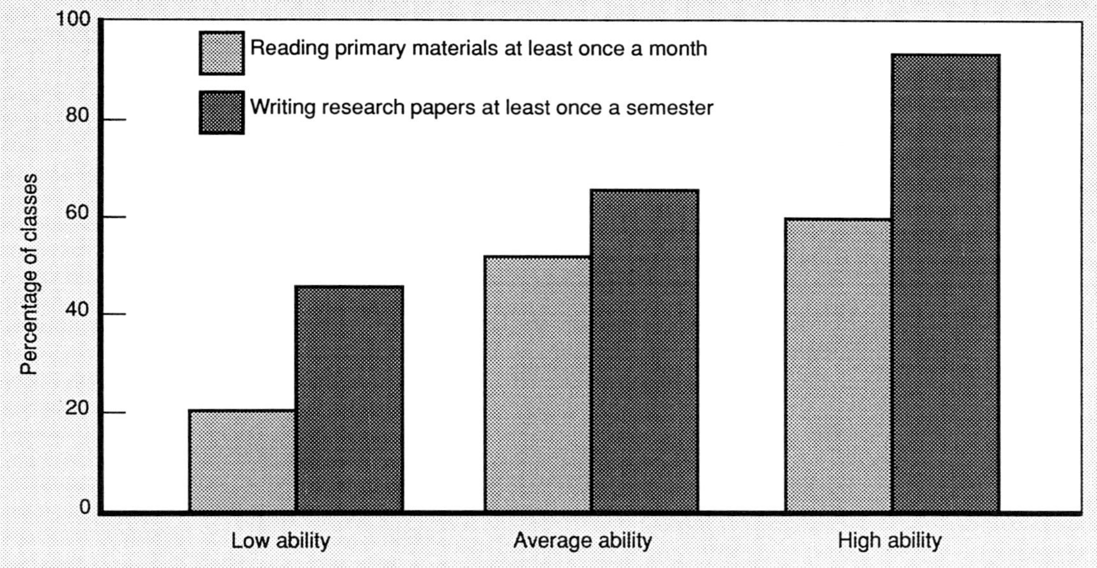

Fig. 4.4—Frequency of assignments, by class ability

On the other hand, whereas topic coverage differentiated among ability levels in the mathematics classes, it did not do so in social studies. The number of periods that high-ability classes spent on a particular topic in U.S. history or government was essentially the same as the time spent by average- and low-ability classes. This finding from the teacher surveys is consistent with school-level interviews that characterized the intended difference among classes for different ability levels to be the depth and manner in which content is presented, not the breadth of coverage, which is supposed to be similar for all classes. The varying effectiveness of different types of measures in describing curricular stratification appears to be valid, given the nature of mathematics and social studies.

One would expect higher levels of knowledge accumulation to characterize more advanced classes in mathematics, while deeper analytical richness is the distinguishing factor in social studies.

... no generic set of statistics should be assumed to apply equally to all courses.

While data on both content and instructional strategies should be collected on all subjects, different measures provide more information about aspects of some courses than others. For example, in social studies, activity and assignment data are key to understanding the nature of instruction received by students of different ability levels. The same data do not provide such information in mathematics, but they are important for monitoring changes in instructional strategies and teachers' responses to reform proposals. Those who report indicator data need to be sensitive to the different types of information that indicators can provide; no generic set of statistics should be assumed to apply equally to the same aspects of all courses.

COURSE OBJECTIVES

In addition to topic coverage and instructional activities, coursework also includes the goals that teachers pursue as they present course content to students and use various instructional strategies. The relative emphasis teachers give to different objectives reveals something about their expectations for a particular course, and their choice of objectives is likely to influence how they configure topics and instructional activities within that course. However, teachers' reports of their course objectives reflect intended behavior and are likely to be less reliable than reports of actual behavior, such as topic coverage and instructional activities. For that reason, course objectives should receive less emphasis when decisions must be made about which data can realistically be collected from a teacher survey.

Although coursework objectives can be a lead indicator of the direction in which coursework and teaching in a particular subject area may be heading, reports of teachers' course objectives should be interpreted cautiously.

Table 4.3 lists 10 teacher objectives for a high school mathematics class and compares the proportions of teachers in the SRA sample reporting a major emphasis on each with the proportions reported in the 1981-82 SIMS sample. The SRA teachers, who were surveyed seven years after the SIMS teachers, appeared to have accepted more of the language of educational reform. The overall emphasis on objectives that appear regularly in the literature on reforming mathematics teaching (e.g., developing a systematic approach to problem-solving, understanding the logical structure of mathematics) was considerably higher for the SRA group than the SIMS groups. Conversely, emphasis on computational speed and accuracy has decreased. This pattern is consistent with reforms that

Table 4.3

PERCENTAGE OF TEACHERS INDICATING A MAJOR EMPHASIS ON A SPECIFIC OBJECTIVE, BY COURSE TYPE

Objective	General Math (N = 33)	Pre-algebra (N = 17)	Algebra I (N = 28)[a]	Overal l Mean	SIMS Grade 8[b]
Understanding mathematical concepts	76	82	100	86	(c)
Knowing facts, principles, and algorithms	70	82	96	83	55
Developing a systematic approach to problem-solving	55	88	96	80	63
Understanding the logical structure of mathematics	60	87	79	75	30
Developing awareness of the importance of mathematics in everyday life	88	47	54	63	61
Developing an attitude of inquiry	42	76	61	60	39
Becoming interested in mathematics	49	71	61	60	45
Understanding the importance of mathematics in basic and applied sciences	42	59	46	49	20
Performing computations with speed and accuracy	55	47	43	48	58
Understanding the nature of proof	12	6	25	14	12

[a]These numbers represent all teachers in the SRA sample who taught a particular course. If teachers taught multiple sections of the same course, they were counted only once, but if they taught two or more different courses, their response for each was counted separately.

[b]Eighth grade teachers' reports of placing relatively more emphasis on a specific objective from data collected as part of the SIMS.

[c]This objective was not included on the SIMS teacher survey.

have been advocated since the early 1980s, although it may be exaggerated by the prevalence of that reform ethos and perhaps by the somewhat different mixture of student populations in the two studies (the SIMS teachers were teaching middle school students, whereas the SRA sample were teaching high school students). We recommend caution in interpreting the changes in teachers' stated objectives because these same teachers report little use of instructional strategies designed to promote such goals. For example, although a high proportion of teachers reported a major emphasis on developing an attitude of inquiry and understanding the importance of mathematics in the basic and applied sciences, activities consistent with those goals (e.g., having students make oral reports, do special projects, or use hands-on materials) were infrequently used. The most frequently employed instructional strategies were more consistent with traditional objectives.

... reports of course objectives should be interpreted in the context of the reforms being advocated at the time data are collected, and they should be compared with teachers' reports of topic coverage and instructional activities.

Table 4.3 also shows that algebra I and pre-algebra courses place greater importance than general mathematics courses on higher-level, critical-thinking objectives (e.g., a systematic approach to problem-solving, understanding the logical structure of mathematics) and objectives dealing with mathematical rigor and understanding (e.g., understanding concepts and knowing facts, principles, and algorithms). In contrast, the major emphasis in general mathematics courses is on fundamental arithmetic skills (i.e., performing computations with speed and accuracy) and the importance of mathematics in everyday living. Even the specific pattern of relative emphasis in pre-algebra is consistent with this course's dual role as a bridge to formal algebraic and geometric methods and as a means of solidifying arithmetic skills and motivating continuing interest in the study of mathematics.

As Table 4.3 illustrates, information on the objectives teachers emphasize does help in differentiating among course levels, and it suggests where particular subject-matter fields may be heading in their instructional content and practices. However, reports of course objectives should be interpreted in the context of the reforms being advocated at the time data are collected, and they should be compared with teachers' reports of topic coverage and instructional activities.

TEACHER QUALIFICATIONS AND TEACHING ASSIGNMENTS

A valid picture of student coursework requires information not only about what is taught and how it is taught, but also about who teaches it. As concern about the quality of the teaching force has grown over the past decade, the federal government and individual states have moved to collect data that would enable them to assess the match between teachers' qualifications and their teaching assignments. The annual Schools and Staffing Survey (SASS) sponsored by the U.S. Department of Education asks a nationally representative sample of teachers about their educational backgrounds (BA major and minor), areas of certification, and years of experience, and also asks for period-by-period descriptions of their classes. Although individual states typically do not collect such detailed information on teachers, a growing number are collecting teacher assignment data that can be linked to state databases on teacher certification status. Twenty-three states can now report the proportion of teachers spending a majority of their time teaching a particular subject who are certified in that subject (Blank and Schilder, 1989).

However, the match between teaching assignments and certification status provides only limited information about teachers' qualifications. Darling-Hammond and Hudson (1989) point out that "the relationship of certification to particular kinds of preparation is uncertain. An uncertified teacher may lack pedagogical courses, subject-area preparation, or student teaching experience, each of which has different implications for a teacher's knowledge and experience base." They recommend that indicators of teachers' subject-matter knowledge will require data on the type of factors included in the national SASS survey, i.e., college major and minor and the number of courses taken in particular subjects.

Different conclusions about the match between teacher qualifications and teaching assignment can be reached when academic major is used as the standard instead of certification. For example, of the 310 mathematics sections in the SRA sample,[8] 83 percent were taught by teachers certified in mathematics, but only 58 percent of the teachers had majored in mathematics or mathematics education.

Figure 4.5 presents a graphic comparison of teacher qualifications, using the two different standards. It also compares teacher qualifications

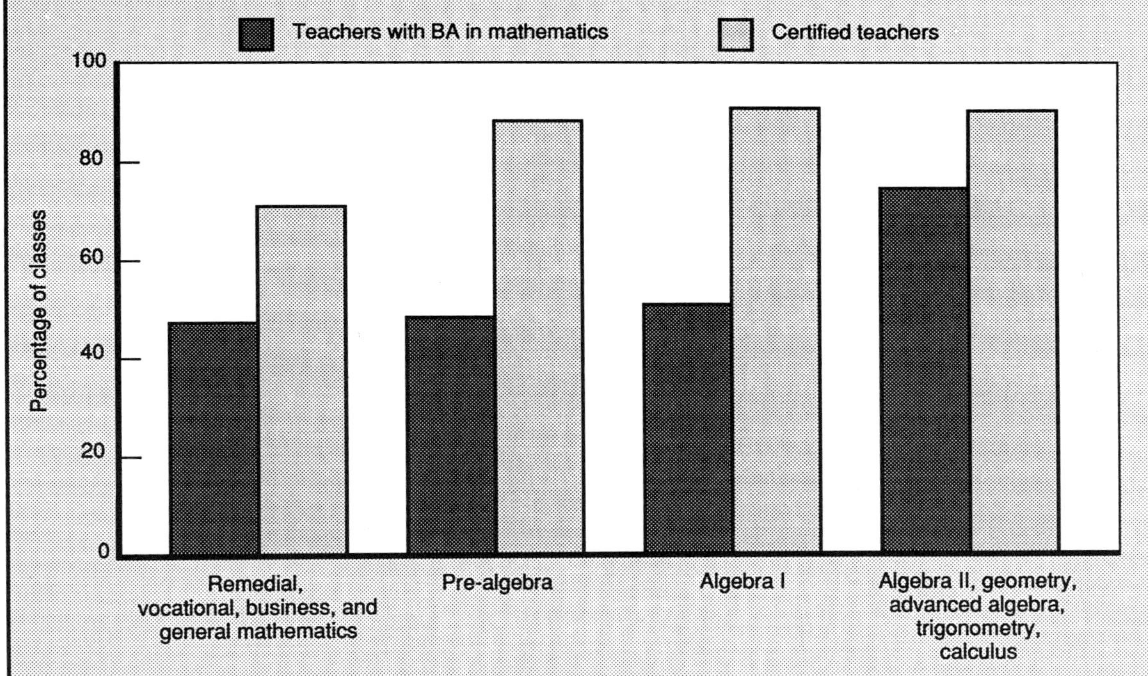

Fig. 4.5—Qualifications of mathematics teachers, by type of course taught

[8]Because of the way data were collected on teacher qualifications, all of the teachers in the seven SRA schools who taught at least one mathematics or social studies course were asked about their qualifications. Thus we were able to collect data on 206 other mathematics sections, in addition to the 104 that were the primary focus of the study.

across different levels of mathematics courses. As might be expected, the classes above algebra I have the highest proportion of teachers who have a BA major in mathematics or mathematics education. However, there is little difference in the proportion of such teachers across the lower three levels.

Years of teaching experience is another criterion by which teacher qualifications are traditionally assessed. Research has shown this measure to be correlated with teacher effectiveness. Although there is some evidence that after too many years, teachers may experience "burnout," or a drop in performance, the consensus is that at least to some point, "experience improves teachers' performance" (Darling-Hammond and Hudson, 1989: 75). Figure 4.6 shows SRA teachers' years of experience across three categories of mathematics classes. Comparison of Figs. 4.5 and 4.6 reveals that experience distinguishes among those who teach various levels of mathematics more than academic qualifications. The most striking finding is the high proportion of novices teaching lower-level mathematics classes: 42 percent of the remedial, vocational, and general mathematics sections are taught by people who have been teach-

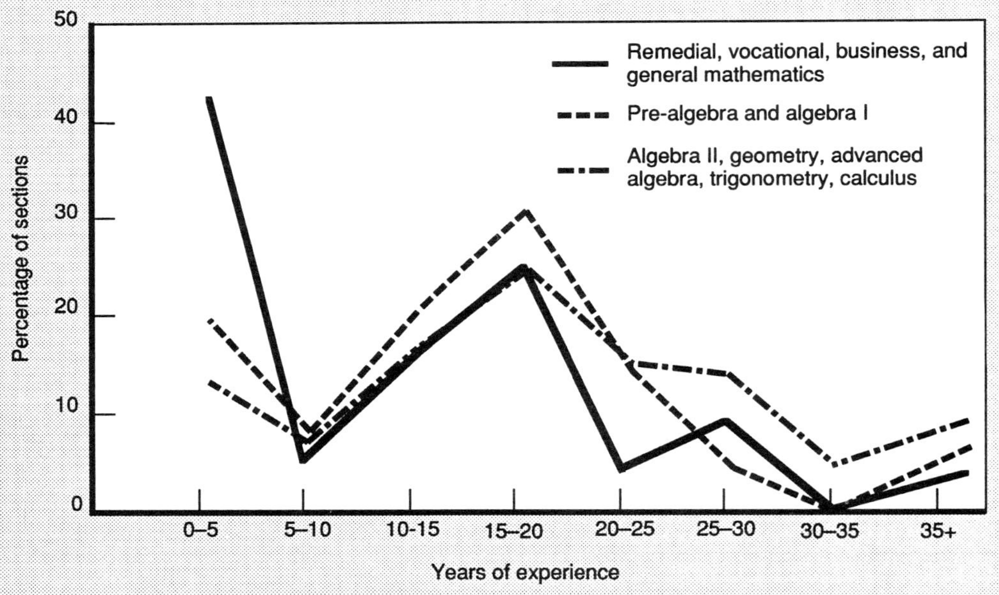

Fig. 4.6—Distribution of mathematics sections, by teachers' years of experience

ing for five years or less, as compared with 19 percent of the pre-algebra and algebra I sections and 13 percent of the classes above algebra I. In contrast, 65 percent of the classes above algebra I are taught by people who have been teaching for more than 15 years; 54 percent of the algebra I and pre-algebra classes and 39 percent of the lower-level mathematics classes are taught by these senior teachers.

Data on teachers have typically been used to describe the current supply of teachers and as a factor in forecasting future demand. However, as these examples illustrate, data on teacher qualifications, experience, and assignments can also be used to develop a picture of student coursework in a state. In addition to comparing the distribution of teacher characteristics across different course levels within one subject area, these data can be used to compare qualifications and experience across different subject areas and across different types of schools and communities. Such information might, for example, be used by policymakers and educators in deciding what kinds of teacher incentives are likely to be most effective for staff development efforts, or in assessing the feasibility of new curricular directions.

A FINAL COMMENT

... one critical task in the indicator design process is deciding what kinds of information are most needed ... and which measures can best be reported in multiple ways to meet those needs.

The indicators discussed in this section illustrate different ways to depict the breadth and depth of student coursework, the distribution of key curricular elements across different course levels, the congruence between the intended and implemented curricula, and teacher characteristics. But these examples are by no means exhaustive of the ways indicator data can be used, nor will they be equally useful to all states and local districts or to all types of policymakers and practitioners. One critical task in the indicator design process is that of deciding what kinds of information are most needed by those in different roles, and which measures can best be reported in multiple ways to meet these differing information needs.

We return to the challenge of reporting indicator data in Section 6, but first we examine some of the strategies that states can use for collecting data on student coursework.

5. DATA COLLECTION STRATEGIES

The tradeoff between ensuring high technical quality and minimizing cost and respondent burden becomes most evident when indicator system designers have to decide which data collection strategies to use. States that are currently collecting information for coursework indicators have selected the least expensive and least burdensome option, school-level statistics categorized by conventional course titles. However, as the technical limitations of these data become more apparent and policymakers demand better information, states will have to seek alternative data collection strategies, even if those strategies entail greater cost and respondent burden. Although such in-depth methods as classroom observation will never be feasible for routine indicator data collection, several of the approaches used in the SRA study represent reasonable alternatives. This section assesses those approaches.

STUDENT SURVEYS VS. TEACHER SURVEYS

One of the least costly and least burdensome methods of collecting data on student coursework is to survey students about what occurred in their classes. Such surveys could be appended to the periodic standardized tests that most states administer. Although students would be asked to spend additional time, the logistical problems would be minimal, since no new scheduling would be required, and the added costs would be marginal.

Students, however, may provide less reliable reports about course content and method of instruction than teachers. Unlike teachers, students do not have lesson plans to refer to in estimating the time spent on different topics, and their recall of content coverage may depend on the extent to which they have mastered that content. Their recollection of class activities and assignments is likely to be more accurate (i.e., they can be expected to remember how often they had to write research papers or whether the teacher lectured every day or several times a week). Student accounts of some activities, however, may be only partly correct because individuals can report on only what they have done, not on what the entire class has done. For example, in a mathematics class, some students might work on problems at the board while others work in small groups or alone at their desks; respondents thus may be able to report on the frequency of only those activities in which they participated most often. Only the teacher can provide a full accounting of the entire range of class activities.

Surveying teachers, however, also has its drawbacks. Most state indicator systems typically do not collect data directly from teachers, or they collect only a nominal amount. A recurring complaint of teachers is that the paperwork burden imposed on them inhibits their ability to teach effectively. In addition, some teachers who perceive that their responses might be used to assess their performance or judge the appropriateness of their teaching strategies may give socially desirable responses rather than accurate reports of what actually occurred in their classrooms.

In the SRA study, we sought to assess these tradeoffs by collecting coursework data from both student and teacher surveys. We concluded that despite their lower cost and burden, student surveys are not reliable substitutes for questionnaire data obtained from teachers, even though there was a reasonable level of agreement between students and teachers on the frequency of classroom activities. Our reasons are threefold.

First, students are unable to answer a number of questions that are critical to understanding the range of curricular offerings across a state—questions about teacher qualifications, the topics covered and whether they were presented as new or reviewed material, and the ability level of the students in a given class. Students can really report only on classroom activities and assignments. And while such information is useful for depicting curricular depth, it tells nothing about curricular breadth, teacher qualifications, or how these factors vary across courses and student ability levels.

Second, our data suggest that for some course levels, student-provided data may be very incomplete. For example, over 90 percent of the students in the SRA sample who took a basic mathematics class either did not report their teachers' names or did not complete the activity grid on their surveys. In contrast, the nonresponse rate for algebra I students was only about 12 percent.

Third, there seems to be no consistent pattern of student disagreement with teachers on the frequency of activities. For example, in U.S. history, 43 percent of the students whose teachers reported small-group activities occurring once or twice a month disagreed, but as many reported that the activity happened more frequently as reported that it happened less often. Similarly, about half the algebra I students agreed with their teachers' estimates of the amount of homework assigned, but of those who disagreed, half reported it requiring more time, and half less. Where disagreements existed across nine algebra I activities, students estimated the frequency to be more than that reported by teachers for five activities and less for four of them.

It is important to note, however, that there was considerable agreement between students and teachers on the most frequently occurring activities. For example, 86 percent of the U.S. history students whose teachers reported lecturing every day agreed; 69 percent of the algebra I students whose teachers reported explaining problems to the entire class almost every day agreed, and 71 percent agreed that teachers reviewed homework problems almost daily.

Despite our strong belief that routine coursework indicator data can best be collected from teachers, we did detect that some teacher responses may be less reliable because of the social desirability pressures mentioned above. Student descriptions of classroom activities in U.S. history generally matched those of their teachers, with two notable exceptions: lecturing and having students read from the textbook in class. About 45 percent of U.S. history teachers claimed to lecture only once or twice a week, while 78 percent of their students reported that the teacher lectured almost every day. Students also reported substantially more reading from the text than their teachers. The majority of U.S. history teachers reported that they required students to read the textbook in class no more than once or twice a month, and a substantial proportion reported giving such assignments even less frequently. But 75 percent of their students reported reading the text in class more often. While these were the only discrepancies that appear to stem from social desirability concerns, they do suggest a need to validate teacher responses periodically with the type of benchmark data described later in this section.

... we conclude that coursework data are best obtained through teacher surveys and that student surveys should be used to obtain information that will increase our understanding of schooling outcomes and student characteristics.

In sum, we conclude that coursework data are best obtained through teacher surveys and that student surveys should be used to obtain information that will increase our understanding of schooling outcomes and student characteristics (e.g., family background, home support, aspirations, schooling preferences). Although student-teacher agreement is high on some of the most common classroom activities, students' inability to provide information on key aspects of the curriculum and differences in the completeness of data across course levels strongly suggest that the tradeoffs in data quality and completeness of teacher reports outweigh the added cost and teacher burden. Burden can be minimized by collecting coursework data once every two or three years and by focusing on a few critical courses in each subject area (e.g., data on ninth and tenth grade mathematics may be more important than data on courses offered in the last two years of high school). Coursework data could also be collected on a cycle; for example, English and social studies could be collected one year, and mathematics and science the next.

The financial cost of collecting coursework data from teacher surveys is negligible. We estimate that a state's costs would amount to less than one dollar per teacher and would probably be lower if the surveys were linked to existing data collection efforts and optical scanners were used for data entry. However, each school would need to devote about a half-day of staff time to ensure that surveys were completed and collected, and individual teachers would need to spend between 30 minutes and 1 hour on the surveys. As noted above, these burdens could be reduced substantially by collecting coursework data less often than student assessment data and by rotating the subject areas on which information is collected.

The major cost lies not in collecting or reporting coursework data, but in indicator development. So much design work has already been done on mathematics indicators that states could simply adapt existing measures to their own information needs, but our research suggests that in other subject areas, states would need to invest in an approximately two-year development effort. This process might involve expert analysis of textbooks, curriculum frameworks, and professional standards, as well as in-depth teacher interviews; these activities would have to be followed by the convening of consensus panels of teachers and subject-matter specialists to reach agreement on the major items to include on teacher surveys. In one sense, then, collecting coursework data through teacher surveys is very cost-efficient and can be quite easily added to a state's existing data collection system. However, the data will not accurately measure what is actually being taught in the state's classrooms unless the state is willing to invest in a thoughtful and well-executed design process.

... collecting coursework data through teacher surveys can be quite easily added to a state's existing data collection system. However, the data will not measure what is actually being taught unless the state invests in a well-executed design process.

BENCHMARK DATA

Interpreting coursework data from state indicator systems and national studies has traditionally been limited by the lack of formal analyses of their validity. Indicator designers have tended to concentrate most of their energy on developing achievement-test items. Despite major advances in the design of background and school process measures, studies have generally developed a few new items and then "borrowed" others from earlier studies or from other states. Little effort has been made to validate these measures by comparing the information they generate with that obtained through alternative measures and data collection procedures. For example, are teachers' reports of curricular goals or content coverage consistent with the material tested and the types of questions asked on their final exams? Are teachers' characterizations of the ability level of their classes consistent with the assignment policies described by school-level officials or the curricular paths of different students that are indicated by transcript analyses?

Ensuring the validity of the inferences drawn from indicator data requires the collection of benchmark data, i.e., data that serve as standards or anchors against which the validity of the routine data can be judged.[1] Benchmark data are more difficult and costly to collect than routine indicator data and can be thought of as a series of deeper probes that do not need to be collected as often or on as large a sample as conventional indicator data.

... ensuring the validity of the inferences drawn from indicator data requires the collection of benchmark data that serve as standards.

Benchmark data can serve four purposes in a state indicator system:

---

[1]*Benchmark data* should not be confused with *baseline data*. Baseline constitutes the first point in a time series, and baseline data are used to estimate change over some period. Baseline comparisons usually use routine indicator data and do not require the special collection procedures of benchmark data.

- As part of the indicator design process, benchmark data can inform the development and evaluation of new measures because the information they generate is much closer to the content and process of instruction than more routine data (e.g., in-depth interviews with teachers or classroom observations vs. teacher surveys), and they are less subject to extraneous influences that limit or compromise routine data (e.g., missing information due to respondents not completing surveys).
- After an indicator system has been operating for some time, benchmark data can be used to assess the extent to which measures have been corrupted by social desirability or policy pressures (e.g., teachers may be reporting classroom behaviors that are consistent with reform policies, while their examinations do not reflect the reforms).
- Benchmark data can provide a context for interpreting trends or unexpected changes in aggregate indicator data (e.g., through school-level case studies).
- Benchmark data can be used in special studies to complement and enhance indicator system data. These studies can explore areas of policy or practitioner concern that indicator data have signaled as problematic (e.g., that curricular opportunities are becoming more unequal in certain types of schools).

Benchmark data may take a variety of forms. In the SRA study, we collected such data by interviewing district and school-level staff, coding student transcripts, and reviewing teachers' syllabi and course materials. Other types of coursework benchmark data collection include regular classroom observations and alternative student assessments administered outside the higher-stakes conditions associated with standardized testing by states.

School-Level Interviews and Case Studies

To obtain benchmark data in this study, we interviewed the principal, the head counselor, and the mathematics and social studies department chairs at each school in the SRA sample. The district-level staff responsible for supervising the high school curriculum were also interviewed. These interviews typically lasted about one hour and were often followed by additional telephone inquiries. Our purpose was to obtain information on the types of students attending each school and whether the composition of the student body had changed recently; the levels of courses offered and whether the curricular differentiation had the same meaning across academic departments; what criteria each school used in assigning students to different courses and sections; how decisions about teacher assignment were made; and how recent state policies may have affected each school's course offerings and instructional practices. We also asked the department chairs to describe in some detail the major differences among the five courses selected for the SRA study in terms of level of difficulty, types of students enrolled, topics covered, instructional materials and strategies, course requirements, and grading practices.

The school-level interviews served several purposes. First, they allowed us to explore the feasibility of collecting coursework data from sources other than teachers in order to reduce the teachers' paperwork burden. We found a reasonable level of agreement across the principal, head counselor, department chairs, and other teachers on how the curriculum is organized in a given school. Differences were most evident in reports about the effects of various policy changes. The teacher surveys and the interview data were in general agreement about how recent state and district policies had influenced curriculum, but administrators tended to perceive a greater impact than the teachers did and were more positive in their assessment of the effects.

The SRA interview data suggest that respondents above the level of department chair cannot report accurately on how curricula vary across student ability levels within a particular department or course. Higher-level respondents tend to underestimate the extent of variation, and even department chairs reported less variation across sections than analysis of the teacher surveys indicated.

A second purpose of school-level interviews was to examine the formal policies that influence curricular stratification within schools. Policymakers who are concerned about differential learning opportunities need information on student assignment policies and how they differ across schools. For example, what role do test scores, grades, teacher recommendations, and student and parent preferences play in assignment decisions? How difficult is it for students to change their course levels, and under what conditions do such shifts occur? We found that reliable information on school policies can be obtained from either the principal or the head counselor, and a survey of such policies might constitute the kind of special study that would enhance indicator data.

Finally, school-level case studies can place indicator data in a richer and more valid context and thus facilitate the interpretation of trends in aggregate data. For example, case studies could identify movements toward more heterogeneous grouping in schools and could indicate how teachers are adjusting to such changes in their content coverage and classroom activities.

Transcript Data

At each school in the SRA sample, we examined the transcripts of students who were ninth graders in 1982 (1983 for Georgia), 1986, and 1988. These three class years were selected because the students who graduated in 1986 in California and 1987 in Georgia were the last to graduate before state-mandated increases in course requirements took effect; the class of 1989 was one of the first classes under the new requirements, and we wanted to examine coursetaking by a class that took U.S. history the prior year; finally, the class of 1991 provided an opportunity to examine the previous year's coursetaking in lower-level mathematics and algebra I.

Each transcript was coded to include student background (gender, ethnicity, birthdate, grade-point average, standardized test scores, and number of absences).[2] The academic level of each course (in mathematics, social studies, English, science, foreign language, vocational education, fine arts, and miscellaneous[3]) was categorized as either:

- *Remedial*—instruction aimed at remediating basic skill deficiencies.
- *Regular/basic*—academic material presented in a manner suitable for students who will end their formal schooling with high school, emphasizing exposure and basic competencies.
- *Applied/vocational*—content focused on students' possible vocational objectives, emphasizing applications in the work setting.
- *Heterogeneous*—material appropriate for students with a variety of abilities and educational objectives.
- *College preparatory*—material that gives students academic skills and breadth of exposure sufficient to prepare them for college-level work.[4]

---

[2]We attempted to collect data on students' socioeconomic status as well, but this effort did not produce consistently reliable information, so the data were not used in any of our analyses. We did obtain data on which students qualified for free or reduced-price lunches. While this measure tends to provide an accurate count of the number of low-income students in rural high schools, it is not reliable for urban high schools because a significant number of students who qualify do not sign up for the program because of embarrassment or for other reasons. We also attempted to obtain information on which students were living in single-parent households. This measure was reasonably reliable for six of the seven sample schools, but the seventh school, as a matter of policy, entered only one parent's name on the student record, whether the child lived with one or two parents.

[3]The miscellaneous category included physical education, driver's education, health and sex education, computer literacy (as opposed to computer programming and computer science classes, which are included in mathematics), and ROTC.

[4]The distinction between the college preparatory and heterogeneous levels is based more on the kinds of students in each class than on course content. Since heterogeneous classes include students who are college-bound, their content must meet the standards for college-preparatory courses but also be appropriate for students of other ability levels and educational aspirations. The major difference between the two course categories is that

- *Honors*—college preparatory content, but enriched or accelerated.
- *Advanced*—material that prepares students for advanced placement (AP) examinations.

Courses were given level designations for two related reasons. First, this enabled us to differentiate among sections of courses such as U.S. history or English in which the same title may mask significant variation in content and academic rigor within individual schools and also across institutions. Second, some course titles have consistent meanings within a particular school but differ across schools. The level designation clarifies the nature of such courses to those outside the school and helps in standardizing course definitions. For example, one school in the SRA sample offered world history at the college preparatory level and geography at the basic level. The difference in subject-matter focus was less important within that school than the fact that the two courses were used to track students who all needed to meet a social studies requirement. In another school, however, a course with the title "world history" was offered to students at both the basic and honors levels. Without the level designation, important differences in course content could go unrecorded in an indicator system based on only standard course titles, particularly in the case of English, history, and social studies courses.[5]

Adding a level designation to a transcript coding scheme presented several difficulties in the SRA transcript analysis. First, the categories were defined to represent different levels of academic rigor in course content. However, content may be confounded with school placement policies if courses are categorized primarily by the ability levels of the students taking them, rather than by their content. A second problem is that while maintaining consistency in course categorizations within schools is fairly easy, keeping that consistency across schools is difficult. A basic course in one school, for example, may not have the same level of academic rigor as the same course in another school. Although we found that the SRA scheme distinguished among courses far better than did standard titles, in a few instances a college preparatory course in one school was closer in content to the basic course offered in another school than to the college preparatory course at that school. Part of the reason for this lack

---

college-preparatory denotes courses which include only students identified as achieving at a level qualifying for college admission, while heterogeneous classes include students with a range of ability levels.

[5]Four additional pieces of information were coded for each course: whether the course was intended for a special population such as handicapped or limited-English-proficiency students; when the course was taken; the grade each student received; and whether the course was taken at the school under study or the credit was transferred from another school.

The coding of this information was based on in-depth interviews with school staff, a review of course handbooks and other materials, and follow-up telephone inquiries, as needed for clarification.

of equivalence is that some schools are more differentiated than others. For example, in a school with no honors or AP classes, the college preparatory courses may have higher levels of academic content than they do in schools that have the additional course levels.

Despite the challenges they present to indicator designers, transcript analyses illustrate two important uses of benchmark data. First, they play an important role in the indicator design process. For example, in the SRA project, transcript analysis was used to develop and test measures of course levels. If these measures were found to be valid in coding transcripts, they could then be tested on other data collection instruments such as teacher surveys. One test of their validity is whether the level of a course a student takes in one year accurately predicts the level of the next year's course, after other relevant factors such as student gender and ethnicity, school attended, standardized test scores, and course grade are taken into consideration. Statistical analyses showed that initial course level, along with test scores, course grades, and school attended, were significant in explaining student course levels from one year to the next.[6] The next step in the indicator development process is to refine the level categories and to include them on a teacher survey to determine whether they have the same meaning for characterizing classes as they do for the transcript data.

Transcript data can also be used in a special-studies component that enhances routine indicator data. For example, teacher surveys allow characterizations of student composition only at the level of sections. If policymakers and educators are interested in which students are taking which courses, transcript analyses can provide a much more complete picture of the learning opportunities afforded different students by using individual-level data. Transcript data can show the curricular paths through high school of vocational as compared with academic students, of minority students, and of boys as compared with girls.

Transcript data can also augment cross-sectional survey and enrollment data by tracing coursetaking patterns over time by student cohorts. This is particularly important in a time of major changes in coursework policies. In the SRA sample, we found that eleventh graders in the pre-reform cohort generally had about the same total years of coursework in each subject area as those in the post-reform cohort. Only for science courses in the California schools did the average number of years taken increase by at least half a year (from an average of 1.5 to 2 years). English was typical of the other subjects: The average number of years

---

[6]The analytical procedures used to test this aspect of the transcript coding scheme's validity are described in the SRA project technical report.

taken by eleventh graders in the Georgia schools remained at 2.9 for both cohorts; it remained at 3.1 for both cohorts in the California schools.

However, some change did occur in the level at which courses were taken. Figure 5.1 shows the trends in English coursetaking in grades 9 through 11 for the two cohorts; similar trends emerged in other subjects as well. The major change was a shift in the distribution of coursework in the California schools. The proportion of students who took all college preparatory and heterogeneous classes increased by one-quarter, to 55 percent of all students. This shift was counterbalanced by a decline in the proportion of students who took some remedial and basic classes. We conclude that in those schools, more students were given the opportunity to take more academically rigorous courses. The shift in the Georgia schools presents a mixed picture. The proportion of students taking all honors and AP courses increased slightly, from 9 to 12 percent, but at the same time, the proportion of students enrolled in all basic and remedial courses also increased, from 29 to 34 percent.

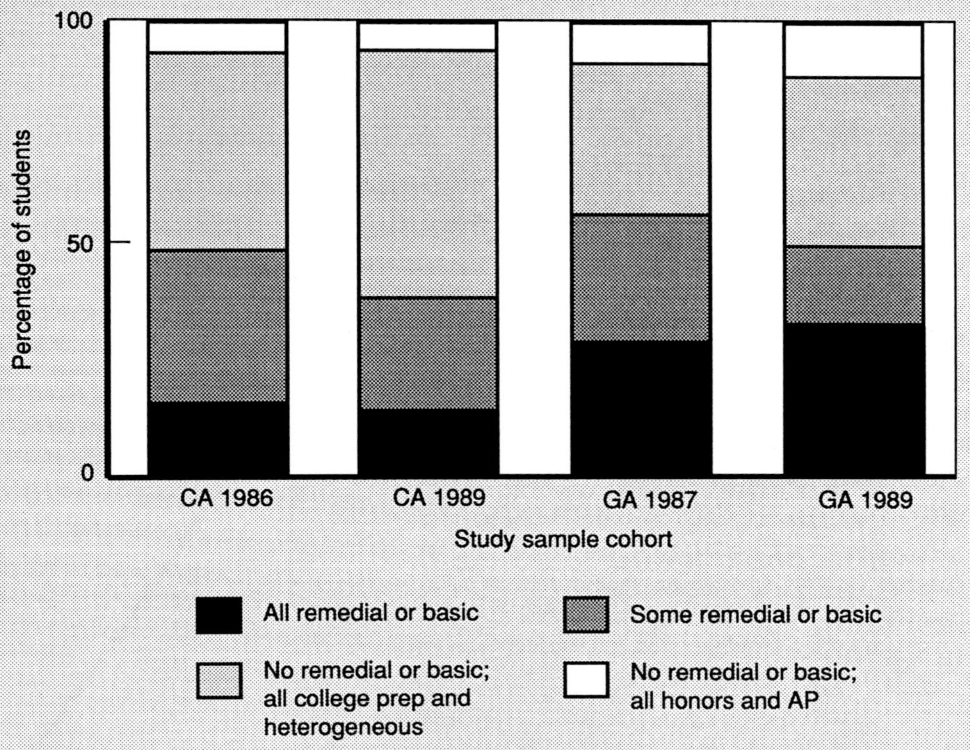

Fig. 5.1—Patterns of coursetaking in English, grades 9 through 11

A simpler statistic that summarizes change in coursetaking over the reform period is the shift in the proportion of students who completed the eleventh grade having taken no mathematics courses at or above the level of algebra I. This is an example of an indicator that is well understood by a variety of audiences and that carries significant information about changes in the academic rigor of student coursework. The proportion of students with this limited mathematics exposure declined in the California schools, from 33 to 25 percent, but in the Georgia schools, it increased from 38 to 45 percent.

The cost of assembling and coding student transcripts prevents their use as a routine data source. Our experience suggests that about four professional staff days per school are required to draw a sample and develop a course classification scheme that is both valid for that particular school and comparable across schools. Assembling and reproducing the transcripts takes about three days of clerical staff time per school, and coding takes from 12 to 15 minutes per transcript.

However, transcript analyses can be an important resource in designing new measures and a cost-efficient way of conducting longitudinal studies that measure change over several student cohorts. With more and more districts now computerizing transcripts, states may be able to make future transcript data collection less costly by encouraging local districts to adopt software that stores the data in a fairly uniform manner and includes some information about course levels.

Course Materials

Data on course materials proved to be the most problematic type of benchmark data. We had originally hoped to collect sample assignments, as well as course syllabi and final examinations. However, a pretest indicated that such an effort would be burdensome to teachers and would be difficult to interpret validly (e.g., the data would not indicate whether the collected assignment was a typical assignment for the third week of the semester or a teacher's "best" or "most difficult" assignment). Consequently, we decided only to request a copy of each surveyed teacher's syllabus (asking how much of the material in it was covered in last year's class) and a copy of the final examination. Even this limited information was difficult to obtain. Only about half of the sampled teachers were able to provide both items, because many do not retain syllabi and examinations from one year to the next.[7] Requesting fi-

[7]An alternative strategy would be to ask teachers about their current-year courses. Unless such a survey were conducted in June, however, the respondents would not be able to report on topic coverage for the entire year or provide a copy of the final examination. Another, more time-consuming strategy would be to ask teachers to submit student assignments and examinations on a regular basis throughout the school year (e.g., once every three or four weeks). This strategy would produce, in effect, teacher portfolios containing accurate data on the coursework actually being delivered to students. However, such data collection would have to extend over most of an academic year.

nal examinations may also overestimate the extent to which teachers rely on the multiple-choice format. In one of the seven schools in the SRA sample, we collected a sample of the tests that teachers administered throughout the year, and we found that students were more likely to be asked to elaborate the steps they used in solving mathematics problems or to answer social studies essay questions on these tests than on final examinations. Forty-seven percent of the 79 final examinations we reviewed were multiple-choice tests, with mathematics and social studies examinations equally likely to be multiple-choice.

Despite the difficulty of collecting data on course materials, such data provide one of the best ways to assess the corruptibility of indicator measures. For example, teacher reports of using instructional strategies or topic coverage geared toward teaching students higher-order skills can be checked by examining the format and content of their examinations. Collecting data on major class projects might also be a way to ascertain whether such teaching is occurring, and it would be subject to fewer problems of interpretation than routine assignments.

Analysis of course materials (i.e., the parts of textbooks that are actually covered in a class, major assignments, and examinations) is probably the most valid way to compare the curriculum actually taught with either professional standards or state curriculum frameworks; valid comparisons often cannot be made with data reported at the topic level. Analyzing course materials can also help in determining the extent to which topic coverage, as reported by teachers, is dictated by the organization of textbooks. Although course material reviews are expensive and time-consuming, they are key to the design of new indicators and to assessing the corruptibility of existing ones. Depending on a state's curriculum and textbook policies, course material analysis might also be a useful focus for special studies linked to the state's indicator system.

The Need for Benchmark Data

At first glance, benchmark data may seem an unnecessary luxury for state indicator systems, and their collection an activity best left to academic researchers. However, we would argue that only with benchmark data can states obtain valid and useful information on student coursework, while still relying on relatively inexpensive data collection strategies such as teacher surveys. The deeper probes required to obtain benchmark data will allow states to validate their indicators over time and to identify where improved measures are needed. Including benchmark data in a system of coursework indicators may also encourage teachers to be more attentive in completing survey questionnaires because they will know that the state takes the information seriously enough to verify it through other sources.

... only with benchmark data can states obtain valid and useful information on student coursework, while relying on inexpensive data collection strategies.

If states decide to close the current gaps in information about student coursework, they will have to balance the expensive data collection traditionally associated with studying curriculum against the standardized, relatively inexpensive methods used for most indicators. A system that relies primarily on teacher surveys and aggregate enrollment statistics, supplemented by periodic benchmark studies, provides such a balance. We recommend that states wishing to collect more extensive data on student coursework should make a significant and continuing investment in benchmark data. Such an investment would require spending about one-quarter of their coursework indicator budgets on these deeper probes.

6. NEXT STEPS FOR STATES

Demands on state governments to generate more and better information about the quality of schooling have grown tremendously over the past decade. As a result, hard choices have to be made about what data can be collected with limited resources. Clearly, the first priority will continue to be indicators of student performance. But a singular focus on schooling outcomes leaves key questions unanswered.

DECIDING TO INVEST IN COURSEWORK INDICATORS

The need to know how learning opportunities vary across schools and students, whether policies to increase the rigor of student coursework have been translated into classroom practice, and how course content and instructional strategies affect student achievement argues for improved coursework indicators. The nation and individual states can set performance goals for their students, but whether those goals are met will depend largely on what is taught and how it is taught in individual schools and classrooms. At present, states lack even the most basic information about these critical elements of schooling. And, as the examples in the preceding sections have illustrated, continued reliance on gross enrollment statistics enumerated by conventional course titles can only mislead policymakers and the public. When courses called algebra I, which most people would assume are reasonably uniform in content, can vary significantly from classroom to classroom, new measures of student coursework are needed.

... indicator design in the service of monitoring educational progress needs to balance both technical and policy considerations.

States must consider the arguments in favor of improved coursework indicators in light of the absolute costs of designing, collecting, analyzing, and reporting new data; the potential opportunity costs of not being able to mount as complete an indicator effort in some other area; and the additional burden that increased data collection would impose on schools and teachers. We believe that the benefits to be gained from this information outweigh the costs, and that by careful design and execution, these costs can be minimized. However, each state must assess its own future information needs, its current data gaps, and the relative importance that policymakers and citizens assign to knowing what schools are teaching.

For states that do decide to invest in coursework indicators, we recommend a six-stage design process. This recommendation is based on our experience with the SRA project and other indicator development efforts. It is also derived from an overriding principle that we believe should guide the design of all educational indicators: Indicator design in the service of monitoring educational progress needs to balance both technical and policy considerations. In practice, this requires a design process that is research-based and policy-sensitive. The six steps outlined below accommodate both sets of requirements. The section concludes with a discussion of several issues that, if not addressed early on, can generate problems in the use of coursework indicators.

THE DESIGN PROCESS

Stage 1. Identify the state's unique information needs. Those needs will determine not only what information is collected, but also how often it is collected, whether it is to include all schools or a sample, and to whom and in what format the data are to be reported. A critical element of any indicator needs assessment is the identification of the major users of the information and the ways in which multiple audiences can be served with the same data. In one sense, the primary audiences for coursework data are the general public (who will probably read the information in their newspapers), state-level elected officials, and education department administrators. However, if coursework data are not meaningful and useful to local educators and parents, the information is not likely to be used by them, nor are they apt to regard its collection seriously. To serve these multiple audiences, data must be reported in different formats and levels of detail. But the need to serve diverse audiences also influences how measures are defined, what data collection strategies are used (e.g., state-level audiences may need information only from a representative sample of schools, but such information would be of little use to individual schools), and the frequency and timing of reports.

Stage 2. Review recent research on indicator design. The growing body of work on indicator design includes analyses of the major studies of schooling and what they imply for the design of improved coursework indicators (Murnane and Raizen, 1988; Oakes and Carey, 1989). This research explores in detail the design standards outlined in Section 2, analyzes the technical reliability and validity issues that must be addressed, and assesses existing indicators on those criteria.

If states decide to collect indicator data on the elementary school curriculum as well, this is the stage at which they would need to think about how those measures and the data collection strategies that underlie them would differ from a coursework focus at the high school level. Although we have not examined this issue in any depth, we are quite certain that it would be necessary to use a different conceptualization and measurement process for elementary-level curriculum indicators than the one we used for high school coursework. Curricular content in elementary schooling is not as clearly divided into separate courses as it is in high schools, and it would be necessary to look for subject-matter content within the content of other subjects (e.g., reading content within social studies, science within reading). Also, in contrast to high schools, where an entire class or section often consists of students in the same ability group, elementary classes typically contain students of different ability levels who are then organized by those ability levels into work groups within the classroom. These instructional groups, several of which operate in each classroom, are the primary unit of analysis for curriculum studies because teachers tailor much of their instruction to these groups (Barr and Dreeben, 1983). Therefore, elementary teachers could not validly report on topic coverage or instructional strategies in the single format used for high school teachers. They would have to report about each instructional group separately or try to determine what proportion of their entire class was exposed to different topics. Finally, elementary students are much less likely than high school students to be a reliable source of information about the instruction they receive. Concerns about access to learning opportunities and the quality of those opportunities call for curriculum indicators at both the elementary and secondary levels, and both require that technical criteria and policy requirements be balanced throughout the design process. But the conceptualization and measurement issues are quite different for each level of schooling, and the schooling research that should guide the development process is also different for each.

Stage 3. Refine and adapt existing indicators. In some areas, such as mathematics topic coverage, instructional activities, and teacher qualifications, states can adapt measures used in the SRA project and studies such as the NELS, NAEP, and SIMS. These measures are not without flaws, but most of them can be remedied with only minor modifications. However, even the most robust measures must be adapted to the state context in which they are used. It is necessary to take into consideration which state policies influence coursework, how schools are organized in a state (e.g., the extent of state as compared with local direction in curricular content, the grade levels at which specific courses are offered or required), and the range of variation in students and classrooms across the state.

Existing coursework measures must also be adapted if they are to be integrated into ongoing information systems. In most states, this means linking coursework data with student assessments and with the collection of data on other elements of schooling, such as resource levels and student and teacher characteristics. The integration of coursework indicators into existing systems will depend on the extent to which they have been defined in ways that draw on other data sources or that piggyback on other routine data collection. For example, it may be possible to obtain some data for an indicator of the match between teacher assignments and qualifications from the state teacher licensure agency. Similarly, states might arrange for teachers to complete coursework surveys while their students are taking the statewide assessment.

Stage 4. Develop new measures. For those areas of coursework where little design work has been done (in other words, subject areas outside mathematics), new measures will have to be developed. This process is likely to take two years for each subject area. Textbooks, curriculum frameworks, and professional standards will have to be reviewed, and in-depth interviews with department chairs and teachers in a variety of schools will be necessary to identify the full range of course objectives, topics, and instructional strategies, and to determine how they are distributed across different types of courses and student ability levels. Finally, consensus panels of teachers and subject-matter experts will have to be convened to ensure that measures are consistent with practitioner and expert judgment, and to select candidate indicators for inclusion on teacher surveys.

There are two strategies that might be used to reduce the development costs in any single state and to spread those costs over a longer time period. Even though indicators must be adapted to the information needs and policy context of individual states, much of the initial development work will be similar. Therefore, states might consider forming consortia (as they are already doing in the assessment area) to collaborate on developing new coursework indicators. Within a single state, development costs can be spread out over several years by focusing on only one or two subject areas at a time. The order in which development occurs might be based on the subject areas emphasized in a state's performance goals or in its curriculum policies.

Stage 5. Devise strategies for piloting the teacher surveys and collecting benchmark data. For the most part, this is a straightforward task, but it does require that decisions be made about the kinds of benchmark data to be collected, collection frequency, and how the data will be used. For example, will benchmark data be collected periodically only to validate teacher survey data and to develop new indicators? Or will it be the subject of full-blown studies that complement routine indicator data but stand on their own with independent conclusions?

Stage 6. Implement data collection. If past experience is any guide, an iterative process involving several rounds of data collection followed by revisions in the measures and instruments will be needed to make the resulting indicators technically valid and understandable to their users; this process will also be needed to establish that data collection procedures are smooth and cost-efficient. Therefore, states that decide to invest in improved coursework measures will have to remain committed for the long haul. A "one-shot" collection of student coursework data will not produce information worth the effort.

AVOIDING PROBLEMS

Those who commission and design new indicators can rarely control the ways in which those indicators are used. Nevertheless, taking into account how similar measures have been used in the past and anticipating how new ones might be used can help avoid problems. The most serious difficulties stem from two simple facts about indicators. First, as they gain significance in the policy world, indicators provide less valid information about what is actually occurring in classrooms—that is, they become corrupted as measures. Second, indicators are powerful levers for changing classroom behavior, but that change often is not what policymakers and indicator designers intended.

Both of these problems are evident in student assessment systems: Tests may no longer measure actual achievement because students have been coached on test content, and the curriculum to which they are exposed has been narrowed to reflect the lower-level skills typically tested. Such unintended consequences are due not so much to the technical quality of assessments as to how results are used. As states have placed more emphasis on student test scores and have attached major policy actions to the results, these "high-stakes" conditions have changed the meaning and effect of assessment data.

It is unlikely that coursework data could ever have the same kind of high stakes attached to their use. But there are situations in which indicators might become corrupted or teaching behavior might change in undesirable ways. We have already suggested that history teachers in the SRA sample may have underestimated the frequency with which they lectured or assigned students textbook reading in class because these activities have been deemphasized in current reform rhetoric. Similarly, teachers might tend to report a greater emphasis on course objectives that happen to be in vogue at a given time. Neither of these examples is particularly serious if a system for collecting benchmark data is in place. Teacher reports about instructional activities can be compared with class assignments, and even within the survey data itself, reports of course objectives can be assessed for consistency with topic coverage and instructional activity reports.

... if coursework indicators are used to compare schools or to assess teacher performance, they will cease to provide valid information and may even distort instructional practices in ways that compromise student learning.

Potentially more serious problems could result if coursework information became another basis on which schools were compared publicly. Just as student test scores are often interpreted out of context, comparing schools on the basis of how much content is covered in different courses or whether instructional strategies are consistent with current reform rhetoric could lead to greater standardization of instructional practices. This possibility represents a very real dilemma for policymakers. A major reason for collecting coursework data is to ensure that course content is consistent with public and professional expectations and that learning opportunities are relatively equal across schools and students. Therefore, state policymakers may want to send a strong signal that they and the public do not want to have algebra classes spending most of their time on arithmetic topics, or that they expect U.S. history students to be given the opportunity to read primary materials and write research papers. The intended effect of that signal would be for educators to change their classroom behavior. But few policymakers would want teachers to have no flexibility in exercising their professional judgment about which instructional strategies are most effective for their own students. The line between expecting research papers to be assigned and an unwarranted standardization of practice can become blurred if coursework data are used in inappropriate ways (e.g., to evaluate schools or individual teachers).

Such problems can be minimized if state officials are clear from the very beginning about the appropriate uses of coursework indicators. These data are most useful for documenting trends, assessing the performance of the overall educational system, identifying and targeting policy solutions, and aiding in local improvement efforts. If they are used to compare schools or to assess teacher performance, they will cease to provide valid information and may even distort instructional practices in ways that compromise student learning.

CONCLUSIONS

Improving the information base on which decisions about educational policy and practice are made is not easy. Designing valid and useful measures takes time; collecting the necessary data imposes financial and other costs; and using indicator data in a constructive way requires considerable thought and planning. While these represent formidable challenges in any type of indicator development, they are particularly demanding in the coursework area because of the need for validation and detailed benchmark data.

Despite these challenges, the price that states will pay for not collecting better coursework data may be even higher. Strategies for attaining performance goals cannot be implemented, classroom learning opportunities cannot be equalized, and policy impacts cannot be effectively monitored if current information gaps are not filled. Indicator development will never have the visibility or political appeal of new policy initiatives aimed at improving schools. Nevertheless, data about what schools are teaching form the cornerstone of those policies, and the constituents of public schooling need that information to continue the work of educational reform.

Appendix

SRA SAMPLE

Number of schools	7
California	
Urban	2
Suburban	1
Rural	1
Georgia	
Suburban	1
Rural	2
Enrollment at smallest school	336
Enrollment at largest three schools	2,000
Number of teachers surveyed	
Mathematics	73
Social studies	63
Response rate (percent)	92
Number of sections in the five course categories examined	
Algebra I and below	86
Algebra II	18
U.S. History	38
U.S. Government	28
Number of students surveyed	
Tenth grade	2,571
Twelfth grade	1,937
Response rate (percent)	75
Number of transcripts coded[a]	
Class of 1986/87[b]	511
Class of 1989	514
Class of 1991	516

[a]Seventy-five transcripts were sampled from the relevant ninth grade class at each school, but about 2 percent were deleted because the transcripts either were sampled from the wrong classes or were not photocopied in their entirety.

[b]The class of 1986 was used for the California schools and the class of 1987 was used for the Georgia schools because they represent the last classes to progress through high school in each state before state-mandated increases in course requirements took effect.

REFERENCES

Barr, R., & Dreeben, R. (1983). *How schools work.* Chicago: University of Chicago Press.

Bennett, W. J. (1988). *American education: Making it work.* Washington, DC: U.S. Department of Education.

Blank, R. K. (1988). *State data available on indicators of science/math education.* Draft paper. Washington, DC: Council of Chief State School Officers.

Blank, R. K., & Schilder, D. (1989). *State-by-state indicators of science and mathematics education: preliminary report.* Washington, DC: Council of Chief State School Officers.

Bureau of Research and Assessment (1986). *The high school experience in Massachusetts* (Publication #14438-74¬500-5-86). MA: Department of Education.

Burstein, L. (Ed.) (Forthcoming). *The IEA study of mathematics III: Student growth and classroom processes in lower secondary schools.* London: Pergamon.

Burstein, L., Aschbacher, P., Chen, Z., Lin, L., & Sen, Q. (1986). *Establishing the content validity of tests designed to serve multiple purposes: Bridging secondary-postsecondary mathematics.* Los Angeles: UCLA Center for the Study of Evaluation.

Burstein, L., Chen Z., & Kim, K-S. (1989). *Analysis of procedures for assessing content coverage and its effects on student achievement.* Los Angeles: UCLA Center for the Study of Evaluation.

Clune, W. H., White, P., & Patterson, J. (1989). *The implementation and effects of high school graduation requirements: First steps toward curricular reform.* New Brunswick, NJ: Center for Policy Research in Education.

Darling-Hammond, L., & Hudson, L. (1989). Teachers and teaching. In R. J. Shavelson, L. M. McDonnell, & J. Oakes (Eds.). *Indicators for monitoring mathematics and science education: A sourcebook.* (pp. 66-95). Santa Monica, CA: The RAND Corporation.

Dossey, J. A., Mullis, I. V. S., Lindquist, M. S., & Chambers, D. (1988, June). *The mathematics report card. Are we measuring up? Trends and achievement based on the 1986 national assessment* (Report No. 17-M-01). Princeton, NJ: Educational Testing Service.

Gamoran, A. (1987). Instructional and institutional effects of ability grouping. *Sociology of Education, 59,* 185-198.

Gamoran, A., & Berends, M. (1987). The effects of stratification in secondary schools: Synthesis of survey and ethnographic research. *Review of Educational Research, 52* (4), 415-435.

Goertz, M. E. (1989). *Course-taking patterns in the 1980s.* New Brunswick, NJ: Center for Policy Research in Education.

Hanson, T. L. (1989). *Curricular change in Dade county 1982-83 to 1986-87: A replication of the PACE study.* New Brunswick, NJ: Center for Policy Research in Education.

Jones, L. V., Davenport, E. C., Bryson, A., Bekhuis, T., & Zwick, R. (1986). Mathematics and science test scores as related to courses taken in high school and other factors. *Journal of Educational Measurement, 23* (3), 197-208.

MacRae, D., Jr. (1985). *Policy indicators.* Chapel Hill, NC: University of North Carolina Press.

McDonnell, L. M. (1989). The policy context. In R. J. Shavelson, L. M. McDonnell, & J. Oakes (Eds.). *Indicators for monitoring mathematics and science education: A sourcebook.* (pp. 241-269). Santa Monica, CA: The RAND Corporation.

McKnight, C. C., Crosswhite, F. J., Dossey, J. A., Kifer, E., Swafford, S. O., Travers, K. J., & Cooney, T. J. (1987). *The underachieving curriculum: Assessing U.S. mathematics from an international perspective.* Champaign, IL: Stipes Publishing.

Murnane, R. J., & Raizen, S. A. (1988). *Improving indicators of the quality of science and mathematics education in grades K-12.* Washington, DC: National Academy Press.

National Council of Teachers of Mathematics. (1989). *Curriculum and evaluation standards for school mathematics.* Reston, VA: Working Groups of the Commission on Standards for School Mathematics of the National Council of Teachers of Mathematics.

Oakes, J. (1985). *Keeping track: How schools structure inequality.* New Haven, CT: Yale University Press.

Oakes, J. (1986). *Educational indicators: A guide for policymakers.* New Brunswick, NJ: Center for Policy Research in Education.

Oakes, J., & Carey, N. (1989). Curriculum. In R. J. Shavelson, L. M. McDonnell, & J. Oakes (Eds.). *Indicators for monitoring mathematics and science education: A sourcebook.* (pp. 96-122). Santa Monica, CA: The RAND Corporation.

Oakes, J., Ormseth, T., Bell, R., & Camp, P. (1990). *Unequal opportunities: The effects of race, social class, and ability grouping on access to science and mathematics education.* Santa Monica, CA: The RAND Corporation.

OERI State Accountability Study Group (1988). *Creating responsible and responsive accountability systems.* Washington, DC: U.S. Department of Education.

Raizen, S. A., & Jones, L. V. (Eds.). (1985). *Indicators of precollege education in science and mathematics: A preliminary review.* Washington, D.C.: National Academy Press.

Shavelson, R. J., McDonnell, L. M., Oakes, J. (Eds.). (1989). *Indicators for monitoring mathematics and science education: A sourcebook.* Santa Monica, CA: The RAND Corporation.